T3-BNY-770

The Global Crisis Makers

Also by Graeme Donald Snooks

ECONOMICS WITHOUT TIME. A Science Blind to the Forces of Historical Change

GLOBAL TRANSITION. A General Theory of Economic Development

LONGRUN DYNAMICS. A General Economic and Political Theory

The Global Crisis Makers

An End to Progress and Liberty?

Graeme Donald Snooks
Coghlan Professor in Economics
Institute of Advanced Studies
Australian National University
Canberra
Australia

First published in Great Britain 2000 by
MACMILLAN PRESS LTD
Houndmills, Basingstoke, Hampshire RG21 6XS and London
Companies and representatives throughout the world

A catalogue record for this book is available from the British Library.

ISBN 0–333–91277–2 hardcover
ISBN 0–333–92967–5 paperback

First published in the United States of America 2000 by
ST. MARTIN'S PRESS, INC.,
Scholarly and Reference Division,
175 Fifth Avenue, New York, N.Y. 10010

ISBN 0–312–23420–1

Library of Congress Cataloging-in-Publication Data
Snooks, G. D. (Graeme Donald)
The global crisis makers : an end to progress and liberty? / Graeme Donald
Snooks.
p. cm.
Includes bibliographical references and index.
ISBN 0–312–23420–1 (cloth)
1. Financial crises. 2. Leadership. 3. Economic policy. 4. Statics and dynamics
(Social sciences) 5. Competition, International. I. Title.

HB3722 .S65   2000
338.9—dc21

00–023346

This book is printed on paper suitable for recycling and made from fully managed and sustained
forest sources.

10   9   8   7   6   5   4   3   2   1
09   08   07   06   05   04   03   02   01   00

Printed and bound in Great Britain by
Antony Rowe Ltd, Chippenham, Wiltshire

To Tim Farmiloe
A publisher without peer

Contents

List of Tables and Figures

Tables

Figures

Preface

A century's end, particularly when it coincides with that of a millennium, usually brings with it warnings of great calamities. Of the end of prosperity, even the end of civilisation. It comes as no surprise, therefore, that the close of both the present century and the second millennium AD is marked by growing anxiety about the future. Many popular writers and intellectuals interpret the economic problems being experienced by major countries such as Japan, Korea, Thailand, Indonesia, Brazil and Russia as signs of a global crisis that will coincide with this changeover in the Western calendar. It seems not to matter that these problems are no different in kind or in severity from those that have afflicted other societies in this and earlier centuries/millennia, or that the timing of these calendar changes is completely arbitrary.

In its fear of the future, modern society is no different from ancient society. Aztec civilisation from 1427 to 1519 is a case in point. End-of-an-era anxiety in the New World was reflected in the New Fire Ceremony conducted in Tenochtitlan, the Aztec capital, every fifty-two years. This ceremony emerged from the Mexica belief about the beginning and end of their world and from the complexity of their calendar. Like all Mesoamericans, the Mexica believed that four world creations, known as the Four Suns, had preceded their own, which they called the Fifth Sun. The Fifth Sun, they believed, was the last Sun. They viewed the passage of time as a circular process, which they measured with both solar and sacred calendars that worked themselves out in an interacting manner over a fifty-two year cycle known as *xiumolpilli* – a bundle of years. Each of the years in a bundle was closely related to similarly named years in other bundles.

Life for the Mexica, therefore, was subject to a precarious process of recurrence. As they believed that the Fifth Sun would eventually collapse, the ending of a bundle of years was regarded as a time of great danger: would the sun be extinguished or would it be renewed for another fifty-two years? The New Fire Ceremony that marked this transition between eras was, therefore, of great significance in the life of the people of Tenochtitlan.

On the eve of a new bundle of years, fires throughout the city were extinguished and the priests went out of the city to a nearby hill to prepare for the great transition. They watched the night sky anxiously to see if the Pleiades (now popularly known as the Seven Sisters) would pass their zenith. If they did the crisis would be over, the sun would rise and a new bundle of years would begin.

With the rising sun, a priest would kindle a fire in the breast of a noble warrior captive, feeding the growing flames with the warrior's own heart and flesh. The fire would then be taken to the temple of Huitzilopochtli, the God of Sun and of War, from where it would be distributed to each local temple, to each priest house, to each warrior house and, finally, to each commoner house. While the priests claimed no control over when the Fifth Sun would end, they assumed responsibility for renewing the Mexica relationship with the divine powers through the New Fire Ceremony. Until this was successfully conducted the future of Tenochtitlan remained in jeopardy. In effect it was a reaffirmation of the conquest strategy that was the basis of Aztec prosperity.

It is not difficult to see the similarities and differences between the ancient and modern attitude towards the future. As in Aztec society, there is considerable anxiety in the modern world about the end of a century/millennium. At the popular level this involves predictions of various calamities and second comings, together with joyful celebrations of the arrival of the new era. We also have our equivalent of ancient priestly rituals, involving predictions by economic 'experts' of global crisis together with the solemn advocacy of austere and painful economic policy, usually in the form of national belt-tightening and deflation that reduces the pace of progress and increases the rate of unemployment. Sacrifices, particularly of Third World countries through the ministrations of the IMF and the World Bank, must be offered up to the economic gods. In difficult times, we are repeatedly told, economic medicine must be painful to be effective.

Yet while the Aztec priests watched the signs and reaffirmed the fundamental dynamic – war and conquest – of their society, our high priests of rationalist economics are involved in undercutting the dynamic strategy – technological change – of the contemporary world. While the ritual performed by Mexica priests had no detrimental effect on their conquest strategy, the neoliberal (or economic rationalist) ritual of modern orthodox economists is, as I argue in later chapters of this book, responsible for derailing the technological strategy and creating an artificial global crisis. While the Mexica priests were crisis watchers, our neoliberal 'priests' are crisis makers.

No doubt there will be a rash of books about impending global crises as we approach the new millennium. What, then, is different about this book? In the first place, it is not a response to the arbitrary nature of the Western calendar. Rather it is an outcome of a long-term investigation of the dynamics of human society that began a decade ago. It is the eighth book in a series on that subject. It will, therefore, be relevant long after the new century/millennium has come and gone.

Second, the global crisis revealed by this study is not to be found in the economic difficulties currently being experienced in East Asia, Brazil or even Russia. These difficulties, it is argued in later chapters, are a normal outcome of the dynamic process at the national level. The global crisis to which I refer is a hidden crisis that has yet to be revealed. It owes its origins to the crisis makers, chief among whom are those orthodox economists who dominate the central banks and bureaucracies of the nations of the world and international organisations such as the OECD, IMF and World Bank. These crisis makers are, as we shall see, responsible for cutting economies down each time they begin to show signs of rapid economic growth. They are able to do so because national governments, suffering from 'the fatal forgetfulness', have abandoned all pretence of strategic leadership – leadership of the strategists who are responsible for driving human society forward.

Third, this book focuses on the real economy, which is responsible for social dynamics, rather than on the financial sector, which plays only a facilitating role. By contrast, other analyses of contemporary global difficulties focus on the so-called 'financial crisis'. This misfocus arises from a totally inadequate approach to the dynamics of human society, together with a desire by financial speculators to convince the rest of us that their problems are our problems and that we should bail them out in times of difficulty.

Fourth, the book's focus on the real economy is the outcome of an entirely new general theory of national and global dynamics. This theory has already been worked out and presented in earlier books in this series on social dynamics. And it has formed the basis for a new policy programme that will overcome the damage inflicted on the global economy by the crisis makers. The failure to construct such a theory is the reason that orthodox economists have blundered so badly. This dynamic-strategy theory, as I call it, is the basis of my distinction between crisis making and crisis breaking, and it accounts for the uniqueness of this book.

Owing to the topical nature of this book, a number of predictions made when the text was being written (1998) had already come to pass by the time the publication process had begun. These include the growing political power of the far right in Europe (particularly in Austria and Switzerland); the signs of an early economic revival in East Asia, which the neoliberal 'experts' told us would take 'decades'; a shift of Socialist-Green policies in Germany back to the neoliberal norm, demonstrating the coercive power of orthodox economics; an increasing incidence of strikes in publicly funded services; and, most importantly of all for the central argument in this book, the increase of interest rates by central banks in the USA, Australia and elsewhere in the neoliberal (economic rationalist) pursuit of the mythical 'monster' of inflation. These outcomes provide additional confirmation of the realism and relevance of the dynamic model employed in this book.

While publishing a number of books with Macmillan Press over the past decade, I have had the good fortune to work with Tim Farmiloe in his capacity as publishing director. Tim is justly famous in the industry for his judgement, decisiveness and efficiency. In addition I found him very encouraging and highly supportive. Publishing will not be the same now that he has retired (late 1999). This book is dedicated to him. I am indebted to Barry Howarth once again for his skills in copy-editing and indexing, to Debbie Phillips for word-processing, and on the publication side to Alison Howson and Keith Povey.

Sevenoaks, Canberra   GRAEME DONALD SNOOKS

Introduction: The Mythical World of the Crisis Makers

The major player in this drama about human society and its future is the global crisis maker. He is the economic expert who is attempting to remake the world in his own image through the promotion of economic rationalist or what I will call neoliberal policy. Essentially it is a drama about the triumph of intellectual ideas over everyday experience; about the elevation of the virtual world over the real world. It is the mythical world of the crisis makers that we will explore in this chapter.

In earlier books I have argued that the role of ideas is to facilitate rather than to drive human progress. Ideas respond to, rather than initiate, desires that are at the centre of the dynamic process. Yet, while ideas are not the cause of progress, they can disrupt it. Indeed, as I will show in this book, a global crisis is emerging today that is a direct result of the flawed ideas of neoliberal economists. These economic experts have constructed a view of reality that is both self-serving and dangerously wrong. And they have been highly successful in convincing most of us that their virtual world *is* our real world.

In turn this has led to the adoption of economic policies in both rich and poor countries that are causing the derailment of the dynamic mechanism of human society. The central argument in this book is that, unless we remove the crisis makers from positions of influence, and unless we adopt alternative policies based on a new understanding of global dynamics, there will be a worldwide collapse that will put an end to the progress and liberty of Western civilisation.

Essentially the neoliberal world is a mythical world. A sense of this critical problem, which will be elaborated in the rest of the book, can be briefly conveyed by considering some of the myths about, and perpetuated by, the global crisis makers. Only by constructing a realistic dynamic theory about human society – something the neoliberals have never been able to do – is it possible to explode these myths.

Some myths about the global crisis

Myth   The global economy is on the verge of a crisis of its own making.

Reality   The apparent 'crisis' to which the neoliberals refer is in reality just part of the normal dynamic process of strategic exploitation and exhaustion experienced by a number of nations in the global community. The late 1990s are no different in this respect from any of the decades in the second half of the twentieth century. A more insidious problem is indeed emerging, but it is the creation of the crisis makers themselves. Could they be trying to divert our attention from their own blundering?

Myth   The current global 'crisis' is the outcome of financial problems in East Asia that have their origins in the corruption and cronyism of political leaders, financiers and wealthy businessmen. It is a crisis that can only be resolved by financial, political and moral reform.

Reality   Financial problems in East Asia are an outcome of the exhaustion or derailment of the dynamic strategies of the countries involved. They are, in other words, the result rather than the cause of real economic problems. Recovery in these countries will only occur when new dynamic strategies replace the old exhausted ones, or where derailed strategies are put back on track. Financial, political, and 'moral' difficulties will resolve themselves as institutions respond to this strategic revitalisation rather than to neoliberal intervention.

Myth   The present global 'crisis' is an Asian crisis. It is the outcome of the 'East Asian meltdown'.

Reality   There is no 'East Asian meltdown', just as earlier there was no 'East Asian miracle'. The mythical sequence of 'miracle' and 'meltdown' is merely the normal process by which dynamic strategies are exploited until they are finally exhausted. After a hiatus – popularly known as a recession/depression – a new strategy will emerge. Each of these aspects of the dynamic process is a new wonder only to an intellectual discipline that has no general dynamic theory.

Myth   World leaders and their economic advisers are deeply concerned about the global crisis.

Reality   Recent (1998) meetings of the G7 and G22 countries to discuss the global 'crisis' were hijacked by representatives of the 'global gamblers' and their backers, the 'global casino financiers'. The global gamblers are those individuals and groups that are speculating in the currencies and paper assets of East Asia. Through their neoliberal supporters they have succeeded in persuading world leaders that a *real* global recession/depression is about to occur. It is not surprising to discover that President Clinton's main economic advisers are former money-market participants (Alan Greenspan and Robert Rubin) and his favourite economic authors are successful market speculators (George Soros).

What is the motivation of the global gamblers? Narrow self-interest. If the speculative boom bursts the global gamblers will be ruined. Hence they are attempting to persuade governments to:

- provide central bank support for hedge-fund speculators such as Long-Term Capital Management (LTCM);
- lower interest rates to support their refinancing schemes;
- grant the International Monetary Fund (IMF) and World Bank greater financial support to prevent the *financial* (rather than real) collapse of East Asia and, more recently, Brazil;
- turn the IMF into a central bank that will support their speculative financial dealings.

It is, in effect, an unholy triple alliance between leading politicians desperately attempting to divert attention from

personal or domestic difficulties, big-time gamblers trying
to prevent a stock market crash, and neoliberal economists
in national (central banks) and international (IMF and
World Bank) organisations who are attempting to tighten
their headlock on the world's rich and poor countries alike.
Clearly the members of this unholy alliance have a vested
interest in persuading us that a global crisis in capitalism
does exist and that it is financial in origin.

Myth   There will be a spillover from the East Asian 'meltdown' to
the rest of the world, probably extending into the new
millennium.

Reality As the downturn in East Asia is, it will be shown, a normal
outcome of the pursuit of a successful dynamic strategy,
there will be no spillover to the rest of the world. Unless,
that is, the world is disoriented by the impact of an exogenous shock as destructive as the First World War. But that is
not the case today. At any point in time there will be
countries such as Japan, Russia and Indonesia that are
caught up in the normal process of strategic exhaustion,
just as there are other countries such as the United States,
Ireland and the Low Countries that are enjoying the fruits
of strategic expansion. In the 1970s, for example, countries
such as Britain, China and those in Latin America were
experiencing similar difficulties. There was no spillover
then and there will be none in the future, *provided we can
break the grip of the neoliberal crisis makers.*

Myth   The recovery of East Asia can be safely left to the IMF and
the World Bank.

Reality Throughout the 1980s and the 1990s the IMF and the World
Bank pursued austere neoliberal policies, known as 'structural
adjustment' programmes, that further deflated and disrupted
Third World countries suffering from strategic exhaustion and
desperately seeking financial support. In effect these organisations are global agents for the crisis makers of the First
World, who are more concerned to extend the influence of
neoliberalism than to assist the economic development of the
Third World. That they do not understand the incompatibility

between neoliberalism and economic development does not diminish the magnitude of this critical problem. Until the IMF and the World Bank permanently reject neoliberalism, they cannot be trusted with the recovery or development of the Third World. To turn the IMF into a world central bank in these circumstances would permanently cripple the global economy and even precipitate the collapse of modern civilisation.

Myth   If Third World countries adopt the democratic system of the Western world, their economies will resume their upward trajectories.

Reality   This widely held view – by even the President of the United States and his advisers – contradicts the obvious fact that Asian countries were no more democratic during the 'miracle' than during the 'meltdown'. It is also at variance with the history of Western civilisation. Economic growth, as will be shown, is a function not of democracy but of the successful pursuit of *any* viable dynamic strategy (including conquest as well as commerce and technological change), while universal democracy is an outcome *only* of the mature phase of the technological strategy. To enforce universal democracy prematurely will only add to the problems of East Asia – problems that would prevent the resumption of rapid economic development. It is essential to realise that the unfolding technological strategy in the Third World will eventually call forth universal democracy.

Myth   There is a 'third way' between capitalism and socialism, or between Keynesianism and neoliberalism, that will lead to national and global revival.

Reality   There are only two ways towards progress and liberty: the virtual way or the real way. The neoliberal way or the strategic way. The wrong way or the right way. It is the strategic way that will be explored in this book.

Some myths about economic experts

Myth   The progress of nations owes much to the influence of economic experts.

Reality   While the material progress of human civilisation has been truly remarkable over the past 11000 years, the economic expert has been with us only a minute fraction of that time. Systematic economic thought emerged only 300 years ago; the foundations of economics were laid down by Adam Smith just over 200 years ago; economics became a separate academic discipline (by breaking the apron strings of history at 'Oxbridge') less than 100 years ago; economists began to exert systematic influence over political decision-making only 60 years ago and they assumed a dominant policy role merely 20 years ago. These facts beg the following questions. How do we account for the economic success of human civilisation for the previous 99.9 per cent of our history? And how do we explain the fact that since the dominance of the economic expert the rate of material progress has diminished? Answers to these questions do not support the myth of the beneficial influence of the economic expert.

Myth   Orthodox economic theory is merely formalised common sense.

Reality   Orthodox economic theory is the very opposite of common sense. It takes at least seven years of intensive full-time training (for the BEc and PhD) to convince young initiates intending to embark on an academic career that they need to deny available evidence of the real world, together with their own innate common sense, in order to adopt the anti-intuitive and artificial rules of the neoliberal game. Only by denying the real world is it possible to believe in the virtual world of neoliberalism. And once they have invested so heavily in acquiring the skills necessary to play this lucrative game, there is no going back. They have too much to lose. That is why the neoliberal approach is impervious to falsifying evidence from the real world.

Myth   Where three orthodox economists are gathered together, there will be at least four different viewpoints.

Reality   Nothing could be further from the truth today than this old joke about economists. Orthodox economics, which provides the intellectual basis of neoliberalism, is monolithic in nature. Neoliberal economists share the same world view and only differ on minor points of interpretation. Tragically they all support the economic rationalist policies that are responsible for the emerging crisis in the world today. Tragically the old joke has backfired.

Myth   The essential contribution of orthodox economics is its ability to model the economy and, thereby, generate restorative policy.

Reality   As human society is in a constant state of flux, it can only be modelled dynamically. The essential failure of orthodox economics is its inability to construct a realistic dynamic model. Its so-called 'growth theory' cannot analyse real-world dynamics because it is constructed from static building blocks borrowed from the neoclassical theory of the firm, which is largely a body of production theory. In effect orthodox economists view society as if it were a factory. And even this deforming view is made up of a series of snapshots rather than a continuous unfolding sequence. It is like hiring a stills photographer to make a movie about modern life by sending him to a local factory. Is it little wonder that neoliberal experts inhabit a fragmented virtual world rather than the dynamic real world populated by the rest of us?

Myth   Neoliberal economists are the champions of free enterprise, non-intervention and liberty.

Reality   To the contrary, neoliberal economists are strong advocates of national and global intervention on a scale that would shock even John Maynard Keynes. At the national level they insist that central banks controlled by fellow neoliberals be totally independent of political – that is, democratic – control, and that they be free to totally disrupt society's dynamic process by eliminating strategic inflation. Governments, they insist, must support this neoliberal intervention by pursuing anti-inflationary fiscal policies. At the global level, neoliberals advocate massive intervention by the IMF and the World Bank – the international agents of neoliberalism – in the economies of the Third World in order to impose deflationary and entirely destructive 'structural adjustment' programmes. Needless to say, this is a perversion of the intentions of the founding fathers (including Keynes) of these institutions at Bretton Woods in 1944. Neoliberalism, despite its ironical name, is not about freedom but about the pursuit by orthodox economic experts of the power and influence that leads to material gain.

Myth   Orthodox economists are responsible for economic growth and, hence, for environmental degradation.

Reality   The denial of this myth is probably the only thing that can be said in favour of orthodox economists. While their rhetoric might be about promoting economic growth, neoliberals actually promote antigrowth policies. Whether they understand this or not. By attacking strategic inflation they are responsible for derailing the dynamic process. They actually pursue the stability of equilibrium rather than the flux of economic growth. Hence antigrowth ecologists such as Paul Ehrlich and David Suzuki have completely missed their mark. Their real targets are the dynamic strategists – the everyman of the modern world – who are responsible for the remarkable progress and liberty of Western civilisation. The radical ecologists also fail to realise that major environmental damage is due not to economic growth but to technological exhaustion. Ecologists, who have more in common with orthodox economists than they realise, need to look at the results rather than the rhetoric of neoliberalism.

Exploding the myths

These are just some of the myths about the global 'crisis' and the crisis makers that are explored and exploded in this book. This is a necessary preliminary step to analysing the hidden crisis and to showing how impending global collapse can be avoided. It has been possible to achieve this in a small book only because it is based on two large trilogies, totalling some 2300 printed pages, which I have published over the past few years. The first of these is the global history trilogy, published by Routledge (London and New York), consisting of:

- *The Dynamic Society. Exploring the sources of global change* (1996);
- *The Ephemeral Civilization. Exploding the myth of social evolution* (1997);
- *The Laws of History* (1998).

The second is the social dynamics trilogy, published by Macmillan/ St Martin's Press (London/New York), consisting of:

- *Economics without Time. A science blind to the forces of historical change* (1993);
- *Longrun Dynamics. A general economic and political theory* (1998);
- *Global Transition. A general theory of economic development* (1999).

All the supporting evidence and arguments for statements made here can be found in those works.

Essentially the argument in this book is that the real global crisis emerging in the world today is a hidden crisis. It has nothing to do with the apparent 'crisis' in East Asia that the neoliberals are trying to convince us will spill over into the rest of the world. Rather, it is a growing disfunction of the global economy brought about by the debilitating neoliberal policies spawned by orthodox economists – by the global crisis makers. Each time the economy begins to grow, the neoliberals, who occupy positions of power in central banks and bureaucracies throughout the Western world, play upon unfounded fears about inflation in order to deliberately derail the dynamic process. I argue that there are only a finite number of times that an economy can be sent crashing to the ground in this way before it will be unable to rise again.

Not only have the crisis makers gained control of the policy-advising organisations of the Western world, they have also taken over the powerful international organisations that claim to provide economic assistance to the Third World. Over the past few decades the IMF and the World Bank have become global agents for neoliberalism. Whenever a Third World country experiences economic difficulties and desperately requires financial assistance, the IMF and World Bank employ their massive economic power to force it to adopt neoliberal 'structural adjustment' programmes in exchange for life-giving funds. But these austere neoliberal policies, involving tight monetary and fiscal policies, merely deflate economies that are already ailing, and succeed only in derailing their dynamic processes. The neoliberal promise of life is cruelly hollow. In this way the neoliberals of the Western world have become global crisis makers.

The purpose of this book is not just to explode this, the most elaborate myth of modern times, but also to analyse the nature of the hidden crisis and to show how its consequences can be side-stepped. As suggested earlier, the rise to power of the neoliberals is a relatively recent event. It is the outcome of a decline in strategic leadership throughout the Western world, which in turn is a consequence of the systematic unfolding of the modern technological strategy that has increased the complexity of sociopolitical structures and decreased the quality of political leadership.

Instead of looking to their strategists, who are responsible for driving social dynamics, Western governments since the late 1970s have turned to the orthodox economic experts to provide both the vision and the method for state action. This is what I call 'the fatal forgetfulness'. Modern governments have forgotten why their institutions emerged at the dawn of human civilisation and why they have been maintained at the taxpayers' expense ever since. They have forgotten that their primary role is to facilitate the objectives of the strategists. The recent collapse of strategic leadership, therefore, has left both national and global economies without overall direction and at the mercy of the fanatical neoliberals. And it is the radical right that will reap the whirlwind.

Having cleared the ground early in the book, later chapters are concerned with the construction of a new approach to the economy. This new strategic way is based on a dynamic vision, on dynamic policy principles, and on dynamic instruments of policy. It shows how the neoliberal experts can be dispensed with, how strategic leadership can be rediscovered, what reforms need to be made to the bureaucracy and the research/higher education system, and what policy instruments should be employed. And in the final chapter the future choices facing our civilisation are considered. It is concluded that if we fail to remove the crisis makers and refuse to adopt the new strategic way, there can be no doubt that, in the immediate future, we will witness an end to progress and liberty throughout the world.

1
The Real Global Crisis

There is much talk today about *the* global crisis. It has become a popular topic in the media, in political circles, among the global gamblers and among economic 'experts'. Evidence for global crisis, we are told, can be seen in the slowdown of the once buoyant Japanese economy, in the sudden transformation of the East Asian 'miracle' into a 'meltdown', in the failure of Russia's transition to an instant market economy, and the reemergence of financial problems in Brazil. Even the sources of buoyancy in the United States are being questioned. Such talk sends the global gamblers into selling frenzies that further weaken the economies of these beleaguered countries.

But are these observed difficulties unique? Are they really the signs of a forthcoming global crisis? Those with any understanding of the past will realise that regional problems of this nature are always with us. Similar difficulties emerged during the 1970s and 1980s in Latin America, China and even the Western world during the OPEC oil 'crisis'. And yet there was no global recession/depression. Such problems emerge regularly in various parts of the world owing to the natural process of strategic exhaustion and, less predictably, to the actions of political extremists (as in Russia and China). Once a new dynamic strategy has been adopted, or once the attack by extremists has settled down, the 'crisis' is resolved and forgotten. Until the next time. For it will be experienced periodically by other societies around the world. This, as I show in my global history trilogy, is a normal part of the dynamics of human society.

Paradoxically, however, a real crisis of global proportions does exist today. But it is not the crisis claimed by other observers. Rather it is a hidden crisis that is the outcome not of the contradictions of capitalism but of those who arrogantly think they can control it. These are the global crisis makers who, surprisingly, are either faceless or bland people: people in private who peddle seductively dangerous ideas, and people in public who use these ideas to shape policy.

These ideas and policies threaten to undercut the long-term viability of rich and poor societies alike. Unlike the more visible economic difficulties, it is a problem that refuses to go away, and will remain even after the more superficial difficulties have been resolved. Its persistence arises from its anonymity. It is a malignancy that is widely regarded as benign. Essentially it is a false vision of what constitutes a healthy society and of the means required to achieve it. This is the real crisis we will face in the new millennium.

The failure of strategic leadership

At the heart of the hidden crisis is a failure of political vision and leadership. Modern Western governments have lost sight of the real reason for their existence, which is to facilitate the unfolding of society's dynamic strategy. This unfolding, which must never be regarded as inevitable, enables the citizens of any society to achieve their key objectives of survival and prosperity. It is for this reason that governments emerged in the earliest civilisations of both the Old and New Worlds, and it is for this reason that governments have been maintained ever since. Until now. In the past few decades, governments of the Western world have relinquished responsibility for promoting and shaping economic development and growth. They have placed our future in the hands of the economic experts in central banks and key bureaucratic departments. This failure of strategic vision and leadership is, as I show, a very modern failure. If it were not so, the modern world would not exist. It is a failure that emerged in a widespread manner only during the second half of the twentieth century.

The burning question is: Why has modern strategic leadership failed? While this issue is examined in detail later in the book, it can be said here that it is an outcome of the growing democratisation of modern society. As I demonstrate in *The Ephemeral Civilization* (1997), the unfolding technological paradigm, which has been under way since the Industrial Revolution, leads not only to economic progress but also to changes in the sociopolitical structure of society. In particular it is responsible for drawing an increasing proportion of the population into the strategic process, which results in both a more equitable distribution of income and a greater participation of the population in the political process.

This growing democratisation strips economic and political power from society's leaders. We need only reflect on the way in which the US Congress has been able to belittle its president. Accordingly the more imaginative and able individuals, who at an earlier time would have entered politics, now seek other more remunerative outlets for their talents. Hence in national politics we are left with individuals whose desires and talents qualify them only to run the existing political system rather than to provide the creative leadership that strategists require to achieve their objectives. These new 'leaders' are content, in other words, to merely occupy the driver's seat in the vehicle of state without ever being tempted to throw the idling engine into gear. In this way they ignore the strategists, who are concerned with material progress, and they seek advice about their role from economic experts, who are concerned merely with the efficiency of this stationary institutional machinery.

The failure of strategic leadership is compounded by the neoliberal advice supplied by these experts. As governments that have lost strategic vision want to appear to be doing something, they adopt policies proposed by economic experts. These experts are members of a highly technical, and thereby inaccessible, intellectual cult known as neoclassical economics. This inaccessibility provides the authority and mystery required by those wishing to predict the future. The process is very similar to that employed by the mystical cults of earlier civilisations – such as the Apollonian cult at Delphi in the ancient world (see my *Economics without Time*, 1993) – that used religious ritual for the same purpose. The Apollonian cult was no less successful in its secular advice than the neoliberal cult, and considerably less dangerous to its society.

The current problem is twofold. Not only does the neoclassical cult possess a flawed view of the world, it has also been able to disguise this through the highly technical nature of its intellectual ritual. Elsewhere – in *Longrun Dynamics* (1998) and *Global Transition* (1999) – I have discussed in detail the problems with the vision, methods and policy of neoclassical economics. Essentially this intellectual cult treats human society as a giant factory dominated by the machine, rather than as an organisation dedicated to the strategic pursuit. Its practitioners focus on the nature of production and on the role played in this by technological change. In effect mainstream economics is a branch of production engineering. And to make matters worse they treat their subject in a static rather than a dynamic way. They insist on viewing our dynamic world – a world in continual flux – through models constructed from static production theory. Accordingly, the orthodox vision of the world is dominated by concepts of equilibrium and order rather than disequilibrium and change.

Such a vision is attractive to politicians with no sense of strategic leadership. Yet even they feel they must exist for some good social purpose. If only they could discover it! What better role could they play than to create order and balance in society? They could not be more mistaken. What they and their neoliberal advisers do not understand is that equilibrium and balance are the very opposite of what is required to maintain the health of any society. As I show in *The Dynamic Society* (1996), the normal healthy condition for any society is disequilibrium and change. Any misguided attempt to force a dynamic society into a static straitjacket will merely damage the viability of that society, perhaps terminally.

The more effective a government is in achieving stasis, the greater will be the eventual crisis. The former USSR is a classic example of this. Governments in Western countries also possess powerful policy armouries, including what I call the policy rules of the four zeros – the pursuit of zero government deficit, zero government debt, zero inflation, and zero market imperfection. If rigorously applied, these neoliberal policy rules will eventually derail a society's dynamic strategy, which is the wellspring of its prosperity and liberty.

In reality it is difficult to enforce these policy rules rigorously despite the desire to do so. Some central banks reluctantly tolerate a rate of inflation of about 2 per cent, which allows a low but precarious rate of economic growth. Whenever the rate of inflation threatens to exceed this second-best target, the monetary authority raises the rate of interest and chokes off the growth process. At a session of the US House Ways and Means Committee on 21 January 1999, for example, Federal Reserve Chairman Alan Greenspan warned that unless growth slowed, through a possible interest rate increase in the near future, there would be a risk of inflation. He concluded that, 'some moderation in economic growth might be required to sustain the expansion'. As I show in *Longrun Dynamics* (1998) and will argue later in this book, a healthy economy requires a rate of inflation of between 3 and 7 per cent per annum to facilitate the unfolding of its dynamic strategy. Continual disruption of this dynamic process through misguided deflationary policies will inevitably lead to crisis and collapse. No leadership at all is better than this type of antistrategic leadership.

The global impact of the crisis makers

Antistrategic policies are currently deforming the dynamic process in both rich and poor countries. In rich countries the outcome of these neoliberal policies depends on the stage reached in the unfolding of individual dynamic strategies. They are particularly vulnerable during the exhaustion phases of these strategies. At this time of hiatus between old and new dynamic strategies, leadership is particularly important. The development of a new strategy requires the combined effort of both government and strategists. Hence, a government that not only fails to provide the leadership necessary to generate a new dynamic strategy but also insists on pursuing deflationary neoliberal policies – the policy of the four zeros – will turn a normal shortrun downturn into a major longrun crisis.

Even a rich country enjoying the rapid expansion of its dynamic strategy will be adversely affected if its government insists on pursuing neoliberal policies. In this unfortunate society, economic growth is seen as a destabilising force because it disturbs the artificial conditions required for neoliberal equilibrium, largely through the agency of inflation that is required to facilitate the dynamic process. As inflation violates the central policy rule of neoliberalism, it must be eliminated. This is done by deflating the economy through monetary (increasing the rate of interest) and fiscal (budgeting for a surplus) policies. Such an approach, even for a society in the full flood of strategic endeavour, will undercut its long-term viability. It will continuously reduce the amount of economic progress achieved, steadily increase the rate of unemployment and bring the expansion phase of society's dynamic strategy to a premature end.

This end will be achieved in a fluctuating manner, as from time to time there will be renewed surges of economic activity. The strategists are not easily constrained. But under relentless pressure from govern-ments determined to enforce neoliberal policies these growth surges will become less regular and less dynamic until, finally, they will cease altogether. An economy caught in this predicament is like an individual struggling to escape an oppressor: each time he attempts to break free his legs are kicked from beneath him and he crashes heavily to the ground, so that on each future occasion he takes longer to struggle to his feet and is more easily driven down again, until at last he refuses to even attempt to rise. The oppressor has achieved his purpose: his victim is now totally compliant; stasis has been achieved.

While it is true that the neoliberal crisis makers will modify their approach during the downturns in this fluctuating process, they regard this as a temporary expedient. As growth slows, inflation falls and unemployment rises, the crisis makers will release their headlock through a reduction in the interest rate, thereby encouraging the strategists to get to their feet once more. But as soon as economic activity turns up again, the neoliberals will complain that economic growth is 'overheating' the economy, and they will warn of the 'monster' of inflation. Then they will choke off the dynamic process by increasing the rate of interest, sending the strategists sprawling once more. This is the nature of the real crisis facing even the richest Western countries. No society enforcing neoliberal policies will be exempt from this end.

Even poor countries are at risk from the crisis makers. They are forced to struggle not only with their own development problems but also against the crisis makers of the rich countries. The crisis makers are evangelists for their cause. And although they walk quietly they carry a very big stick. That stick is the economic power wielded by the IMF and the World Bank, which are the international agents of neoliberalism. Third World governments, unlike their First World counterparts, still know what is in their best interests – to facilitate the objectives of the strategists with whom these are closely associated. Of course the situation in the Third World is more clear cut because the strategists are a relatively small and distinctive group, and because their leaders have usually risen from their ranks. These leaders understand that economic growth will facilitate their best interests, and that policies of stability will merely be self-defeating. They understand that their future depends on a dynamic rather than a static society.

The problem facing Third World leaders, particularly during times of internal difficulties, is that they are forced to contend with those powerful agents of neoliberalism, the IMF and the World Bank. At such times the crisis makers of the First World can distort economic policy in the Third World by threatening to withhold much needed funding unless the hopeful recipients adopt neoliberal 'structural adjustment' policies. These are the familiar antigrowth policies – the policies of the four zeros – of the First World that disrupt, even derail, the vulnerable dynamic strategies of the Third World.

The former Second World is also at risk. For much of the twentieth century these communist countries struggled to compete with or even to dominate the West. They failed to do so, as I show in *The Ephemeral Civilization* (1997), because, although their command system was first-rate at oppressing potential strategists and extracting surpluses from the people, it was not very effective in generating sustained economic progress. The opposite was true in the West, where progress and liberty flourished. Under Cold War conditions the collapse of the Second World was inevitable. Their only hope of survival, as their moribund command system ground to a halt, was to replace their antistrategic tactics with the strategic pursuit of the West. They had, in other words, to make the transition from a command to a market system.

Paradoxically the only 'ally' of the Soviet bloc was its old enemy. Under the guise of enlightened self-interest, the West offered its vanquished foe not the dynamic advice it desperately needed but the static advice that would complicate its transition. It was given neoliberal advice, not strategic advice. This advice, which was provided by private consultants, national governments, the IMF and the World Bank, had to be adopted if the former Soviet bloc countries were to receive the funds required for transition. For example, in November 1998 the new German chancellor, Gerhard Schröder, announced that further investment funds would not be provided to Russia unless it continued to pursue IMF structural adjustment programmes.

Wanting advice on how to achieve progress and liberty, the former Second World was given advice that would ensure economic collapse and political chaos. The irony is that, while strategists in the First World have been capable of generating progress and liberty, its neoliberal experts have been unable to understand the process by which this has been achieved. Is it little wonder that the Russian transition has broken down and the country is on the verge of political chaos? This transition will only resume once Russia is able to reject neoliberal advice and to provide the leadership required to facilitate the objectives of its strategists. Until then the Russian people will be caught between an untenable past and an unachievable future.

The real crisis exposed

What, then, is the essence of the real global crisis? Essentially it is an endemic crisis of the modern world that has emerged from a struggle between the crisis makers and the strategists. At this stage the crisis makers have the upper hand. Each time the strategists get into stride they are struck down, thereby endangering the stability of the national and global economies. This outcome raises two important questions. Why have modern leaders turned against the strategists? And how can this critically dangerous situation be reversed?

Modern leaders have turned from the strategists to the neoliberal experts because they have lost their strategic vision and they feel more comfortable with stasis than with change. This, I have argued, is an outcome of the democratisation process driven by the unfolding industrial technological paradigm. The economic and political power of leaders and their people are inversely related. As the power of the people increases, so the more imaginative and able individuals are driven from politics into the corporate sector. While this has had a devastating effect on the quality of political leadership, owing to the small numbers involved, it has failed to generate a compensating increase in the vigour of the business world.

With the decline in the quality of political leadership has come an increase in the demand for expert technical advice. Some of this demand may have been generated by the growing complexity of our modern technological society, but it is largely an outcome of the growing failure of strategic leadership. Modern political leaders seek advice not only on technical problems, which is only to be expected as the world becomes more complex, but also on what *their* objectives should be and how they should attempt to achieve them. Of course successful strategic leaders in the past have always sought practical advice on how best to implement their strategic policies, but never 'philosophical' advice on their role and objectives. This is why there were no economic theorists or economic theory in the pre-modern world, only practical 'how to do it' instructors and manuals (see *Economics without Time*, 1993).

There is an additional reason for the declining political sympathy for strategists. Once again it is an outcome of the unfolding techno-logical paradigm. As the paradigm unfolds, the socioeconomic struc-ture of society becomes increasingly complex and fragmented. Many pressure groups emerge, each demanding that their special interests be attended to. Some of these are profit-seeking strategists, but many others are rent-seeking antistrategists. The problem is that the grow-ing complexity of society makes it increasingly difficult to distin-guish between these two categories. This is a matter of critical importance because the strategists drive our dynamic system, whereas the antistrategists undermine it. During earlier phases in the unfold-ing of our modern technological paradigm, when the socioeconomic structure was less complex, it was easier to distinguish between these categories.

Conclusions

In brief, as the process of democratisation proceeds, the complexity of the sociopolitical structure of contemporary society increases, the quality of political leadership declines and the role of the expert increases. These outcomes of the unfolding technological paradigm reinforce each other, leading to a shift of alliances from political leader and strategist to political leader and expert. Ultimately this dynamic process generates a failure of strategic leadership, the isola-tion and alienation of the strategist and the emergence of serious national and global crisis.

Of course what we need to know is whether the growing global crisis can be halted and the failure of strategic leadership overcome without reversing the desirable process of democratisation. In theory there are two ways in which this outcome could be achieved: either by modifying the political structure to encourage the reentry into politics of more imaginative and able individuals, or by replacing the static neoliberal vision that has no role for government leadership with a new dynamic vision that focuses on strategic leadership. In reality it is highly unlikely that an advanced democracy will desire, or even be able, to invest more power and authority in its political leadership. Consequently, it is imperative that we displace orthodox economic theory with what I have called – in *Longrun Dynamics* and *Global Transition* – dynamic-strategy theory.

Dynamic-strategy theory, it is argued in Chapters 3 and 8, provides a realistic vision of human society. It does so because it is based not on unrealistic assumptions, as in the case of orthodox theory, but on a systematic study of the rise and fall of real societies. Failure to change our vision will cause a deepening of the global crisis that may lead to the collapse of the modern technological paradigm and, hence, to the fall of Western civilisation. At the dawn of a new century and a new millennium we face a critical choice, which must be made soon.

2
Who are the Crisis Makers?

To understand the real global crisis we need to identify the crisis makers and to discover the secret of their remarkable rise to power. The rise of the crisis makers is a very recent phenomenon, one which must be reversed soon if the future of Western civilisation is to be secured. The fundamental irony of the modern world is that although we have discovered the technological strategy that would have prevented the fall of Rome, that very strategy is changing the sociopolitical structure of our world in a way that is endangering our civilisation. Just when we have discovered the source of eternal progress and liberty, we have delivered our future into the hands of the crisis makers. The most important question of our age is: Will modern civilisation follow Rome into oblivion?

Identifying the crisis makers

The global crisis makers are a set of interacting professional groups who benefit materially from their mutual relationship. They include the economic experts who have engineered the present antistrategic world vision known as economic rationalism or neoliberalism, the policy makers who have forced this vision on us, and the popular interpreters who have persuaded us that this vision is as good as it gets. This is not to imply that there is a conspiracy between these three groups. They, like the rest of us, are merely responding opportunistically to the dynamic forces of our time. Our misfortune is that the crisis makers have misinterpreted those forces. Hence the challenge facing us here is to correctly interpret these forces and to redirect them before it is too late.

Before examining the dynamic forces that have given rise to the crisis makers we need to understand more about them. I will argue that the economic experts are orthodox neoclassical economists, the policy makers are risk-averse politicians, and the popular interpreters are financial journalists. Of course there are individual exceptions to this argument in all three groups, but, as usual, the majority rules.

The economic expert

The economist is a late arrival on the intellectual scene. While mathematicians, historians and philosophers were to be found in the earliest civilisations, political economists did not emerge until the late seventeenth century. Even so, the foundations of classical economics were not laid down until the publication of Adam Smith's *The Wealth of Nations* in 1776, over two hundred years ago. And for a century after that the great Western economic thinkers could be numbered on the fingers of one hand – Thomas Robert Malthus, David Ricardo, Karl Marx and John Stuart Mill. Indeed there was no profession of economics until some time after Alfred Marshall established an economic tripos – by finally breaking the apron strings of history – at Cambridge in 1904. Even this new profession had little systematic influence on political thinking until the 1930s, and only then because of the combined impact of the Great Depression and the remarkable intellectual powers of John Maynard Keynes. The influence of the economics profession increased exponentially after the Second World War as governments sought technical advice on rebuilding their war-torn economies and in addressing the issue of economic development in the Third World. But it was not until the last quarter of the twentieth century that orthodox economists gained a stranglehold on economic policy in rich and poor countries alike.

We should not, therefore, fall into the trap of thinking that economists have always possessed the influence they enjoy today. And within this profession the rise of the neoclassicists, referred to as neoliberals in this book, have been even more recent. The early political economy of Smith, Malthus, Ricardo, Marx and Mill dealt with the broader issues of economic growth and income distribution throughout society, whereas neoclassical economics, which emerged from the 1870s onwards under the influence of Stanley Jevons, Carl

Menger, Léon Walras and Alfred Marshall, dealt with the more narrowly focused theory of the firm. This was the new microeconomics or, more correctly, the economics of small-scale production. The neoclassical vision of society, therefore, is of a factory rather than a dynamic social organisation.

It is an unfortunate fact that this supply-side or 'productionist' faction in economics grew more influential as the twentieth century progressed. The only challenge to their intellectual and practical dominance was made by the demand-side macroeconomics of J. M. Keynes during the four decades following the publication of his influential book *The General Theory of Employment, Interest and Money* in 1936. But this influence was not to last, as the neoclassicists were determined to reinterpret Keynesian macroeconomics in terms of their own mathematically formulated production theory. By the mid 1970s the 'productionists' had taken Keynes apart, distorted his vision and thrown him away. They were able to do this because even Keynes had insisted on building his demand-side theory on a static and deductive foundation. Even Keynes failed to understand the true dynamic nature of human society and the method (induction) required to explore it. But the final, and disingenuous, excuse for abandoning Keynes entirely was the stagflation that emerged from the OPEC oil crisis during the 1970s. I say disingenuous because stagflation – the simultaneous increase in both prices and unemployment – can be explained quite simply in non-neoclassical terms. Since the 1970s, therefore, the neoclassicists have occupied centre stage both in the economics profession and in policy advice.

What is the neoclassical vision that for the past generation has been forced on the world? Essentially it is, as already suggested, a vision of human society as a factory dominated by the machine. The objectives of society are interpreted in terms of physical output that is viewed as an outcome of the aggregate production function defined in terms of physical inputs (land, capital and labour) and technology. It is a production or supply-side relationship expressed in static rather than dynamic terms.

The ideal neoliberal society is one in which production is maximised subject to its physical and human resources. The key catch-cry is not dynamic progress but static efficiency. In this ideal society no one can be made better off without making someone worse off. This is a state of efficiency known as Pareto optimality, and it is a state of equilibrium that will be departed from only through an exogenous (external) shock. The end to which human society is striving, the neoliberals tell us, is one of order, balance and stability – in a word, stasis. Change is merely a means to achieve this end – a shift from the imperfect to the perfect state. Neoliberal policy, therefore, is intended to assist in the achievement of the most efficient (equilibrium) state, largely through the removal of market imperfections. In effect they wish to make the real world resemble their static models.

The economic experts who provide the vision for the crisis makers include academic economists, bureaucratic economists and political advisers. Academic economists are responsible both for refining the neoclassical vision and the methods required to implement it, and for passing these ideas on to their students who have been traditionally employed in bureaucratic departments (such as treasury/exchequer, finance, trade, employment and so on), central banks and international organisations such as the OECD, the IMF and the World Bank. Hence the official policy-making departments of Western countries, together with their international agents in the Third World, are staffed by economic experts from the same tertiary educational organisations. They are the products of neoliberal training.

Central banks in particular are major fortresses of neoliberalism. These institutions, which are staffed by neoclassical monetarists, are not responsible to the strategists because they have, in the main, been granted a monopoly over monetary policy. It is interesting that Western governments managed to wrest control of monetary policy from the private banks after the Great Depression only to surrender it to the neoliberals after the OPEC oil crisis. Hence a major instrument of economic policy has been transferred from the strategists who drive the dynamic society to grey-suited fanatical ideologues who have little understanding of this process.

Less risk-averse souls eschew the bureaucracy to take up more precarious positions in the employ of ministers of the state as private advisers. Unfortunately even their advice is very similar to that provided by the bureaucracy. All economic experts come from the same neoclassical schools. A well-known Australian treasurer (and later Labor prime minister) explained, when asked in a television documentary (following his retirement) to justify 'the recession we had to have' of the early 1990s, that he had received the same advice – to increase interest rates to avoid trade deficits and inflation – from every quarter, including the Treasury, the Reserve Bank, his own staff, and the academics. The crisis makers have a common vision.

The policy makers

Today's policy makers are risk-averse politicians with little or no expertise in economics. While the latter could be an advantage, provided they were prepared to look to the strategist rather than to the expert, it means that they are unable to evaluate the neoclassical vision owing to the highly technical ritual in which it is embedded. Politicians with tertiary qualifications usually achieve them in law and political science. Accordingly they have some understanding of legal and political institutions, but little of the workings of the economy. Worse, they are predisposed to thinking of economic processes in institutional terms. In these circumstances their economic vision and policies are shaped by an army of personal advisers, public officials and private consultants who, as suggested earlier, are all imbued with deforming neoliberal ideas. And this advice usually falls on fertile ground. Most senior politicians today, for reasons discussed below, have a penchant for order, balance and stasis. Hence the neoliberal view of the world appeals to them despite the obvious fact that they do not understand the underlying theoretical models. They are easy converts to neoliberal policy – the policy of the four zeros.

Today's political leaders have lost sight of the strategic leadership that characterised successful societies and civilisations of the past – even the very recent past. They have forgotten that the reason for the emergence of the state in all past societies was to facilitate the objectives of the strategists. And in their forgetfulness they have turned from the strategists to the economic experts to define their purpose. True, they have discovered a new role, but it is a role that threatens to destroy modern society. They are currently attempting to force the dynamic aspirations of our strategists into a straitjacket of order, balance and equilibrium. If they succeed, the long-term viability of Western civilisation will be thrown into jeopardy.

From time to time, particularly during periods of high unemployment, contemporary political leaders feel uneasy about the neoliberal approach. They are aware that some sections of the electorate have been alienated by their austere policies. While they accept the neoliberal dictum that there can be no gain without pain, they usually become anxious about the declining political support and are tempted to intervene in the economy, either directly by undertaking public works or indirectly by subsidising private activity in certain sensitive areas. This brings them into conflict with their neoliberal advisers, who are determined to minimise government interference in the economy. The outcome is a clash between the unrealistic neoliberal ideal and the fundamental desire for political survival. When governments insist on the introduction of interventionist policies, often after bureaucratic heads have rolled, it is a matter of pork-barrel politics rather than strategic leadership. If these governments manage to weather the political storm they revert once more to neoliberal policies because, having lost sight of the role of strategic leadership, there is no other way.

In these circumstances, to whom can the strategists turn? All the main political parties, which are subject to the same economic advice, have adopted similar neoliberal policies. Hence while it is possible in a democracy to change political parties at the ballot box, it is not always possible to change economic policies. At the present time there is only one economic vision and one set of policies to implement it. This has the potential to create dangerous political situations in Western countries.

In their frustration, strategists will turn increasingly to radical parties, particularly those on the right, in an effort to find strategic leadership – just as they did in Germany in the early 1930s. This is seen most clearly in a few Western European countries (Austria, France, Belgium) and in the remarkable rise of the One Nation Party in Australia in the late 1990s. If the main political parties in other Western countries continue to pursue neoliberal policies, the global crisis will grow and a new wave of fascist parties will be created. Only the adoption of strategic policies by mainstream parties will prevent this occurring. These issues are explored in greater detail in Chapter 6.

The popular interpreters

Neoclassical economics is a highly technical intellectual cult. Its mysteries are understood only by a small number of initiated members who are required to pass through at least seven years of intensive technical training in mathematically formulated abstract theory – years during which common-sense observations about the dynamic nature of the real world are suppressed in favour of a highly unrealistic mathematical game. The unreality of this game lies not in the abstraction – even realistic theory abstracts from day-to-day experience – but in the narrowness and triviality of its focus. It focuses on the chaff of human endeavour rather than the grain. Scholars who are unwilling to suspend disbelief in this narrowly artificial game turn to other more realistic intellectual activities. The majority, however, appear content just to play the game of neoliberalism.

Not surprisingly, academic economists concerned with the technicalities of their game find it impossible to communicate with the general public, which has more down-to-earth preoccupations. And more common sense. But if political leaders are to apply their neoliberal policies, the general public must be persuaded to accept the vision of the economic expert. That is the job of the financial journalist, who has some knowledge of the neoclassical cult and is experienced in breaking down complex ideas into simple notions. These popular interpreters accept the conventional economic wisdom without understanding that it is only an artificial game. They wax lyrical about the panacea offered by neoliberalism, and they defend it from common-sensical popular attack. They also screen out any alternative paradigms that might arise from minority groups of intellectuals. The public rarely receives any information through the popular media about insightful challenges to economic orthodoxy. Instead the popular interpreters merely repeat what they hear at economic conferences, what they read in less technical working papers and journals, and what they extract from 'reliable' cult gurus.

Probably the most remarkable example of neoliberal hagiography is a front page article in *The Times* (15 February 1999) on Alan Greenspan (chairman of the US Federal Reserve), Robert Rubin (secretary of the US Treasury), and Larry Summers (deputy secretary of the US Treasury), entitled 'The Committee to Save the World'. This article paints a glowing picture of three white knights who, through their financial interventions (a central neoliberal inconsistency) at the national and global levels, have been successful in 'saving the world' from collapse. We are told with bated breath that these three men from the world of finance and academia, who have 'out-grown ideology' despite their 'faith in markets' (another inconsistency), are not only 'inventing a 21st century financial system' but are single-handedly responsible for 'fighting off one collapse after another' and preventing 'a near thing becoming a disaster'. This has been possible due to their 'intellectual honesty' and their success in 'defending their economic policy from political meddling'. This is no less than the 'great (neoliberal) man' view of history.

In this way the popular interpreters help to persuade the educated public of the 'truth' of neoliberalism. And in this they have been remarkably successful. One need only listen to the spokespersons of those well-meaning social organisations committed to the welfare of the disadvantaged. While they wish to see a reduction in the rate of unemployment and an increase in the provision of welfare, they feel compelled to agree with the popular interpreters that this can be achieved only in a society that adopts the austere policy of the four zeros. And this in spite of their common sense telling them that the very reverse is true. They have been persuaded by the popular interpreters to the common-sense absurdity that only in a world in equilibrium will their objectives be achieved. As I will argue later, these neoliberal policies will place a stranglehold on our dynamic society that will generate a world in which only the economically powerful will gain, at the expense of the weak.

The popular interpreters are in a powerful position. To challenge the orthodoxy that they champion is to invite public ridicule. Few are willing to risk this. The educated layperson eventually learns to abandon common sense and to adopt the neoliberal position, despite the inability of governments to solve the economic and social problems that concern them. And what our social leaders are persuaded to accept, the rest of the community is forced to follow. We are all taught by the popular interpreters to repeat the neoliberal mantras: 'fight inflation', 'budget for a surplus', 'liquidate public assets to eliminate public debt', 'create a level playing field', 'abandon trade protection and embrace globalisation'. It is all a triumph of artifice over common sense. Only eccentric individuals without a well-developed sense of survival dare to demur.

The rise of the crisis makers

How do we account for the rise of the crisis maker? Is there a connection between the decline of strategic leadership and the rise of the economic expert? Why is the emergence of the economics profession in general and of neoclassicism in particular such a recent phenomenon? To answer these questions it is essential to understand the dynamic mechanism of modern society. It is a subject that has been systematically explored in my global history and social dynamics trilogies.

Both the rise of the economic expert and the decline in strategic leadership are outcomes of the wider global dynamic process that has been under way since the British Industrial Revolution was forged between 1780 and 1830 – a revolution that is spreading steadily around the globe. This is what I mean by the unfolding industrial technological paradigm. As this strategic unfolding has taken place, a larger proportion of the population in most advanced nations, and a larger proportion of the world's nations, have been drawn into the dynamic strategy of technological change. This process, which must never be regarded as inevitable, has delivered two highly desirable outcomes – increased prosperity and greater liberty – and two counterproductive outcomes – a decline in strategic leadership and the rise of the economic expert. The rise of the expert is considered in the rest of this chapter, and the decline in strategic leadership is explored in Chapter 5.

The late and great Joseph Schumpeter, in his authoritative *History of Economic Analysis* (1954), puzzled over the absence of any body of systematic economic thought in the ancient world. He was puzzled because Greek and Roman thinkers have always dazzled us with their achievements in the fields of mathematics, philosophy and history. Clearly, analytical economics would not have been beyond them. But he had no solution to this puzzle. In *Economics without Time* (1993), I argued that as the civilisations of the ancient world were at least as successful as our own – ours has yet to last as long – then economic theory was not a necessary condition for global economic success. Had there been a demand for economic theory in the ancient world, there can be no doubt that it would have been forthcoming. I further claimed that the reason it was not required by the ancients was that they already possessed a perfectly adequate method for making policy decisions – the use of economic history. In other words they based their decisions on a systematic analysis of past economic experience rather than on abstract deductive models. This implies that economic history was not the offspring of economics, as most believe, but rather its much older (by a few millennia) sibling. Why then, I asked, did modern society bother to develop and apply deductive economic theory to policy making? At the time (1993), I concluded that it was a response to the growing complexity of economic decision making in modern society.

A subsequent, more detailed study of the ancient world, under-taken in my global history trilogy (1996–98), made it clear to me that this answer was totally inadequate for at least two reasons. First, ancient Rome was larger and more economically complex than the British economy of the seventeenth and eighteenth centuries, when classical political economy became a major intellectual discipline. For example, the population of the city of Rome at its peak was in the vicinity of one million people, whereas that of London in 1750 was only 675 000. Second, economic complexity is a technical rather than an intellectual matter. The ancient world generated tons of technical accounts of how to manage landed estates, how to run mercantile businesses, how to conduct military campaigns and how to administer vast empires, but it possessed no economic treatises because its leaders did not need to be told what their objectives should be or how they should achieve them. The ruling elite of ancient civilisations knew what was in their best interest and what their dynamic strategy should be. Today, economics is called upon to show not how business or bureaucracy should be conducted but what the objectives of society should be and how they should be achieved. The irony is that the neoclassical theory of the firm is actu-ally useless in showing businessmen how to conduct their businesses.

The penny finally dropped once I had developed the dynamic-strategy model to explain the rise and fall of human civilisations. As outlined earlier, the unfolding technological paradigm has increased prosperity and liberty, but only at the cost of a decline in strategic vision and leadership. In turn this has led to a growing demand for economic experts who can define and implement an alternative vision. The economic expert, therefore, is a natural outcome of the modern dynamic process. But was it inevitable that the dominant economic experts would have a fatally flawed neoliberal vision?

About one hundred years ago a great intellectual battle called the *Methodenstreit*, or battle of the methods, took place between neoclassical deductivists and the historical economists (or inductivists) in both Germany and Britain. It was a battle that the historicists lost, owing largely to the less critical global circumstances of the late nineteenth century in comparison with those of the late twentieth century. In other words, as economic survival did not depend on the outcome of this intellectual battle, the neoclassical technicians were able to outmanoeuvre the realists, as one might in a game of chess.

In the late nineteenth century the neoclassical economists were able to treat economics not as a realistic study but as an intellectual game. They were able to do so because the outcome of their intellectual game had few implications for their societies. Governments in Western Europe at that time were still able to appreciate their strategic role in facilitating the objectives of their dynamic strategists and did not need the advice of economic experts. In these historical circumstances, intellectual victory favoured the 'gameplayers', who were the neoclassicists.

My argument in *Economics without Time* (1993) is that 'gameplayers' have an advantage over 'realists' because what matters in the intellectual world, as opposed to the real world, is not how realistic your analysis is but how many articles can be placed in the profession's 'best' journals. In this respect the neoclassicists have it all over the historicists. As neoclassical economics is a deductive–mathematical discipline, its practitioners reach their intellectual peak much earlier and are able to generate more journal articles than the historicists, who require considerable experience to reach intellectual maturity and who, owing to the greater complexity of reality reconstruction, write books rather than articles. It is, therefore, not surprising that the gameplayers receive more rapid promotion than the realists and, within a relatively short time, come to dominate the profession. Had realistic problem-solving been more important than mere technical brilliance, the *Methodenstreit* would have had an entirely different outcome. Today the emerging real global crisis, which is placing greater importance on solving real rather than artificial problems, may turn the tables in the coming battle between historicists and neoliberals. This book is intended as the opening shot.

Conclusions

The fact that the crisis makers have been thrown up by the unfolding technological paradigm does not mean that the process is irreversible. It may be necessary to accept a decline in the average quality of leadership as a cost of democracy, but we must not be content with a powerful body of professional advisers who are more interested in game-playing than in solving real problems. Intellectual game-playing is a luxury that we can no longer afford now that the real global crisis is approaching.

Gameplayers have little value in the real world of internationally competitive business. They flourish only in protected enclaves such as universities and bureaucracies. It is perhaps ironic that under the influence of neoliberal gameplayers, governments throughout the world have reduced the public funding of these enclaves, with the result that the wider demand for gameplayers has declined. Perhaps they are not as clever as they like to think. In response to changing market demand, university students are moving into more relevant areas of study, such as finance and business. And a siege mentality is developing in academic economics. At last the ground is being prepared for the reform of the social sciences (discussed in Chapter 8) that must be undertaken.

But while the gameplayers are declining in numbers they still hold the policy high ground. They still hold a monopoly over the intellectual cult of economic prediction. In order to break the monopoly of the crisis makers we need to formulate a new and realistic vision of human society. That too is part of the purpose of this book.

3
What is Really Happening Globally?

The real global crisis, I argue in the opening chapter, is a hidden crisis. It is the consequence not of the slowdown in East Asia but of the neoliberal policies of the Western world. The economic problems that emerged in various parts of the world during the 1990s are a normal outcome of the global dynamic process. There is nothing unique about these problems and without the hidden crisis they will not lead to global depression. Yet this argument begs the questions: What is the global process that has produced the problems of East Asia and how will they be resolved? To answer these questions I briefly review the orthodox story and then I outline the real story – the strategic story.

The orthodox story

The orthodox story of the global crisis is a confused story. It is confused because neoclassical economics has no way of coming to grips with real dynamic societies. Most of the large body of mathematically formulated theory is concerned with small static issues rather than big dynamic issues. It is concerned, for example, with what happens to the price and output of a commodity if a tax of a certain size is imposed by the government *in an unchanging world*. And for questions of social statics such as this, neoclassical economics is a useful and powerful tool of analysis, provided only an approximate answer is required. The main problem is that all the big questions are a matter of social dynamics, on which neoclassical economics has very little to say. What, then, is the point of an arcane science that can tell us how the price of popcorn is determined, but has nothing useful to say about the nature and determinants of global dynamics?

The best that neoclassical economics has been able to achieve in the critically important field of dynamics is to construct so-called 'growth theory' from static microeconomic (production theory) building blocks. For reasons I discuss at length in *Longrun Dynamics* (1998) and *Global Transition* (1999), growth theory does not even begin to replicate the dynamic processes of real societies. Hence orthodox economists are unable to make any systematic sense of the changing nature of the global economy or of its constituent societies. Their analysis of the current 'global crisis', therefore, is largely intuitive and ad hoc, owing more to value judgments than to objective science.

To begin with, orthodox economists are confused about the nature of the global 'crisis', even at the most superficial level. Not only have they completely missed the fact that there is more to the global crisis than meets the eye, they have even misread the nature of the visible global problems. Most economic experts identify the central global problem with difficulties that have emerged in financial markets in East Asia, Russia and Brazil.

The Economist, that self-confident organ of neoliberalism, is more concerned with the 'turmoil in financial markets' than with what is happening in the real global economy. Indeed it does not readily distinguish between the two. It tells us, for example, that the 'financial turmoil'

> began in Asia a year or so ago, when currency crises there led to a sharp increase in emerging market bond yields. . . . The trouble spread to developed economies in April, when investment banks' bond-trading desks started to lose money for the first time since 1994. . . . Things became much worse in August after the Russian government devalued. . . . The news of LTCM's [Long-Term Capital Management's] troubles and its rescue was the last straw (17 October 1998, pp. 21–3).

This sequence of financial events is supposed to have increased the perceived riskiness of assets, which led banks to sell at a time when there were few buyers, thereby reducing liquidity. *The Economist* forecasts that this could lead to a 'credit crunch' and a downturn in economic activity throughout the world. This is a bit like attempting to analyse the reasons for the sinking of the *Titanic* by describing the growing panic of passengers rushing around the decks, clambering into lifeboats and splashing into the ice-cold Atlantic as the listing ship begins its terrible descent.

The Economist is not alone in this interpretation of past and future global events. In early December 1998 the World Bank, through its chief economist Professor Joseph Stiglitz, warned that sharp stock market falls in the US or Europe, or a continuing pause in international capital flows, could precipitate a recession. The solution, the World Bank claims, is to restrict or tax 'hot money' capital flows. Once again, therefore, we are told by the economic experts that the global crisis is a financial crisis.

The Economist's and World Bank's analysis is fairly typical of the orthodox supply-side approach. Orthodox economists focus on capital-supplying institutions such as banks and stock exchanges, and on the speculators, sometimes euphemistically called 'arbitrageurs', who contribute to market volatility. In the process the so-called financial crisis is identified with depression in the real economy. Parallels are drawn, erroneously, with the role of the Wall Street crash at the outset of the Great Depression of the 1930s. For example, Japan's current problems, which have led to negative growth, are blamed on its unsound financial institutions, 'crony capitalism' and the failure of the government to undertake supply-side reforms. The Southeast Asian crisis is seen in similar terms. All this is reflected in the agenda for recent (1998) meetings of the G7 and G22, which resembled jamborees for financial experts and central bankers.

Even when the real economy is mentioned, it is usually in the context of the old supply-side standbys of 'overproduction' or 'over-investment'. An obvious problem with the concept of overproduction, which neoliberals are unable to explain satisfactorily, is that it implies that producers (or investors) are irrational. Why otherwise would they continue to churn out goods and services that cannot be sold? This irrationality has much in common with the metaphysical mission of Karl Marx's capitalist, whom he describes in the following terms: 'Accumulation for accumulation's sake, production for production's sake: by this formula classical economy expressed the historical mission of the bourgeoisie'. As I show in *The Laws of History* (1998), Marx's dynamic model, which had a predetermined outcome, was driven not by the forces of reality but by the laws of destiny. Could it be that supply-side orthodox economists unknow-ingly also subscribe to similar metaphysical forces? If they believe in the concept of overproduction, they must.

The bottom line is that orthodox economists do not know what is really happening globally or how to resolve the problems that periodically arise. Why? Because they do not possess a realistic general dynamic theory. What, you ask, about orthodox 'new' growth theory, which is also called 'endogenous' growth theory? What, indeed? From time to time our leading politicians are asked this question by the popular interpreters in a manner that suggests this theory actually has something to say about the dynamics of human society. It does not. In this instance the ignorance of our leaders is truly bliss.

Essentially the problem with the new growth theory – as I show in *Longrun Dynamics* (1998) and *Global Transition* (1999) – is that it was not designed to analyse the dynamics of real societies. Rather than asking the common-sensical question 'What is the dynamics of human society and how can we model it?' the new growth theorists ask 'How can we use our existing theory about the hypothetical factory (microeconomics) to build mathematical models that generate outcomes that can satisfy a technical definition of economic growth (such as "convergence to the steady state")'? These are two very different questions and they lead to entirely different answers.

The new growth theory, like microeconomics more generally, assumes that human society is a giant factory dominated by the machine. This is not a novel assumption, however, as it is shared with the nineteenth-century founders of both the radical and neoclassical traditions in economics – Karl Marx and Alfred Marshall. Yet the new growth theorists act as though they believe they have stumbled across something entirely new. They make a great fuss about their attempt to 'endogenise' technological change (the machine), which they characterise as R&D, in their productionist (or factory) models of human society. The wheel is always being reinvented in a discipline with no understanding of its own history.

There are four matters to note about the new growth theory. First, technological change in this model is merely an assumption imposed on an earlier (mid 1950s) version of the neoclassical growth model (known as the Solow–Swan model). It does not arise from the opera-tion of their basic model, as it does from my dynamic-strategy model. The reason is that new growth theory is constructed deductively (that is, logically from initial assumptions) rather than inductively (that is, generalising from observations of the dynamics of real societies).

Second, there is nothing new about the recognition of the role played by technological change and human capital in the growth process. It has been documented empirically since economic historians (for example, Arnold Toynbee Snr) began in the mid to late nineteenth-century to examine the Industrial Revolution; and it has been theorised about since the time of Karl Marx (1867) and Joseph Schumpeter (1912). What took the neoclassicists so long to catch up with the past?

Third, as discussed in *Global Transition* (1999), the new growth theorists have actually endogenised the *wrong* variable. Technological change is only one of the supply-side **strategic instruments** that respond to strategic demand. It is merely what I call a **surplus-generating medium** – a medium for translating the dynamic impulse into increased income – in the same way that conquest and commerce were in the ancient world. Had the ancients built a growth model by endogenising conquest they would have been no further from, or indeed closer to, the truth about dynamics than the new growth theorists. Both have omitted the very mechanism that is, and has always been, responsible for the dynamics of human society. This is the **strategic pursuit** which, as discussed later in this chapter, is at the very centre of my dynamic-strategy model. The inappropriately named 'endogenous' growth theory, on the other hand, lacks any self-starting or self-maintaining dynamic mechanism.

Finally, the new growth theory fails to model both economic and political change. While it views human society through the production processes of a highly abstract factory (or farm or office), it fails to encompass even the power relationships on the factory floor, let alone those throughout society. Dissatisfaction in orthodox ranks with this omission has led to the 'new political economy', which attempts to explain political decision making in terms of economic rationality. But this too is a product of deductive neoclassical economics and, as a result, fails to provide a realistic interpretation of the role and functions of political institutions, particularly in a dynamic setting. Further, the new political economy is unable to link up with the new growth theory. There is no escaping the fact that neoclassical economics has no economic and political theory of human dynamics. In view of this, it defies reason that some 'new' economic historians (those who have traded their common sense for the neoliberal vision) are attempting to employ the new growth model to examine historical dynamics – to use an antihistorical model to reconstruct history!

The real story

The real story about global dynamics can be told only by entering the one true laboratory of the social sciences – the labyrinth of history. Only through a systematic study of the way real societies have risen and fallen can we get to grips with social dynamics. A realistic general dynamic theory can only be constructed using the inductive method. Why? Because the deductivists have had three centuries in which to develop the critically important discipline of social dynamics and the best they can come up with is the utterly sterile new growth theory. It is time to see what the inductivists can do.

In *Longrun Dynamics* (1998) and *Global Transition* (1999) I employed the inductive method – generalising from a systematic study of history – to construct a general economic and political theory that can explain not only the dynamics of rich countries but also the global process by which poor countries are drawn into the vortex of economic transition. This theory, which I call the dynamic-strategy theory, consists of interacting models of economic growth, economic fluctuations, economic development and sociopolitical change. In the remainder of this chapter I will briefly outline this new theory, together with the way it can be used to interpret the global situation and to make sensible predictions about the future. The real story, we will discover, is a strategic story.

A new model of economic growth

The dynamic-strategy theory treats human society as an organisation devoted to the strategic pursuit. By this I mean that human society is driven by the biologically determined desire of **materialist man** (very different to the artificial *homo economicus* of neoclassical economics) to survive and prosper by investing in the most effective available dynamic strategy. Feedback about strategic effectiveness is provided by the continuously changing material standards of living. If these standards decline, then those who invest in a particular dynamic strategy – the **strategists** – will pressure (even remove) their political representatives to provide more effective **strategic leadership**, and if this fails they will explore the possibility of adopting a new strategy.

Throughout history these dynamic strategies have included only four basic possibilities: family multiplication (procreation and migration), conquest, commerce and technological change. The last of these, technological change, which is the dynamic strategy of the modern era, has included a variety of substrategies, such as the pioneering industrialisation programme adopted by Britain after 1780, and the microelectronic/biotechnological programme pursued by contemporary society (to name only two).

The exploration of strategic opportunities by materialist man, which is what I mean by the strategic pursuit, drives the unfolding dynamic strategy. This unfolding process, which must never be regarded as inevitable, takes place through a sequence of linear waves lasting approximately 300 years (the 'great' waves) and 50 years (the 'long' waves). And it gives rise to synchronised changes in **strategic demand** and **strategic confidence**.

Strategic demand is the total demand of all strategists in a society for the physical, intellectual and institutional inputs required to exploit changing strategic opportunities, while strategic confidence is the state of mind that generates trust and enables cooperative investment and effort in the dominant dynamic strategy. Strategic confidence is only maintained while the dominant dynamic strategy is unfolding successfully: once the dynamic strategy or its substrategy is derailed or exhausted, strategic confidence will decline rapidly and, hence, societal trust and cooperation will collapse. In this way the dynamic process involves an interaction between the forces of competition and cooperation.

Strategic demand and strategic confidence are key concepts in my dynamic theory. They give rise to the increase in investment, saving, labour skills (human capital) and ideas of all sorts, and to the changing institutions and organisations that characterise a successful dynamic strategy and substrategy. This strategic demand–response mechanism is orchestrated by rising prices (**strategic inflation**), which provide the necessary motivation and information for economic change. Strategic inflation, which must be distinguished from **nonstrategic inflation** resulting from external shocks (for example, the OPEC oil crisis of the 1970s) and policy errors, is a stable and non-accelerating function of economic growth. In other words long-run economic growth cannot be achieved without strategic inflation. And as a systematic study of history shows, viable societies are able to sustain rapid rates of economic growth without running the risk of hyperinflation. Hyperinflation only takes place in societies, such as Germany after the First World War, that have had their dynamic strategies derailed by endogenous shocks or antistrategic policies.

While this dynamic theory of human society contains a self-starting and self-maintaining process, economic growth will continue only until the dynamic substrategy/strategy has been exhausted. From this point in time, strategic demand and strategic confidence will begin to decline and society's funds will be transferred from old strategic (profit-seeking) uses to antistrategic (rent-seeking) and speculative activities. This is, however, only a temporary expedient. Once rigor mortis has spread throughout the old dynamic substrategy/ strategy, it is only a matter of time before the economy turns down, the speculative boom bursts and the economy is left in the hands of rent-seekers chasing an ever-diminishing surplus. In other words, financial excesses and rent-seeking emerge on a widespread basis only when strategic opportunities fall away, and these excesses will be reversed only when a new and successful dynamic strategy begins to unfold.

Meanwhile our society will experience a **strategic hiatus**, usually called a recession/depression, between the old and the new substrategies/strategies. This hiatus is potentially more serious when it falls between two strategies (such as between Britain's commerce and technological strategies in the mid-eighteenth century) than between two substrategies (such as in Japan in the 1990s). Some societies, such as Rome, were unable to make this transition and therefore ceased to exist.

We can illustrate the working of the dynamic-strategy model for rich countries by considering the Great Depression of the 1930s, which began in the United States and, owing to the unusually severe problems that were inflicted on the world economy by the First World War and its disastrous peace settlement, spread rapidly to the rest of the globe. As I show in *The Ephemeral Civilization* (1997), the Great Depression was an outcome of the exhaustion of the technological substrategy that the United States had been pursuing since the 1890s. This substrategy involved the development of large-scale forms of industrial production and distribution in order to exploit the American mega-market created during the nineteenth century through the expansion of the western frontier.

The gradual exhaustion of the US technological substrategy during the 1920s generated a number of outcomes that are often, quite wrongly, regarded as independent causes of the Great Depression. Of these the first is the growing saturation of the domestic market for consumer durables. Contrary to orthodox argument, this was due not to 'underconsumption' or 'overproduction' but to an exhaustion of the domestic market (given the state of the existing technological strategy), which had provided the United States with its strategic opportunities over the previous fifty years. Second, the increasing degree of speculation on Wall Street and other stock exchanges in the 1920s was not an independent causal factor in the depression but merely an outcome of the exhaustion of US strategic opportunities. In an effort to continue earning supernormal profits, many former strategists turned to speculative activities, where they were joined by swarms of followers. The continuing shift in the balance between strategic activities (profit-seeking) and speculative ventures (rent-seeking) during the process of strategic exhaustion was fed by a high, if artificial, level of **gamblers' confidence** which replaced strategic confidence. Only when the dynamic strategy crashed did even this gamblers' confidence collapse, bursting the giant bubble of speculation and sweeping the gamblers away.

The downturn and contraction of the US economy, therefore, was the outcome of the collapse of the old technological substrategy, which had been closely linked to the exploitation of the giant domestic market through mass production and mass distribution. This strategic exhaustion and crisis led in quick succession to a sharp reduction in strategic demand for labour, capital, technological ideas and money balances; to the decline and collapse of strategic confidence and hence business expectations; and to the collapse of gamblers' confidence and associated speculative activity, most conspicuously and spectacularly on Wall Street. None of these responsive variables, as is usually claimed, was an independent cause of the Great Depression, merely a passive part of the strategic contractionary process.

In normal circumstances the US downturn would have had only a limited impact on the rest of the world and, as a result, would have been much less severe in the United States itself. Until the subsequent emergence of a new substrategy, the United States would have experienced only a modest decline in real GDP and employment, probably on the scale exhibited by Japan in the 1990s. The international economy during the 1920s, however, was anything but normal. Indeed it was highly unstable due to three sets of extraordinary forces: an imbalance in the Atlantic economy, particularly in commodity and capital flows, as a result of the First World War and the consequent reparations; an incomplete baton change in world financial leadership and responsibility between Britain, the pioneering industrial nation, and the United States, the first industrial mega-state; and a reduction in international specialisation, which led to a state-sponsored build-up of commodity stocks. The US downturn was merely the final blow that broke the back of the global economy.

In the United States, recovery from depression depended on the development of a new technological substrategy. This required the redirection of its existing mass production/distribution approach from the domestic to the international market. It was this strategic redirection, rather than the Second World War, which led to the United States abandoning its isolationist foreign policy. The recovery, which proceeded in a fluctuating manner throughout the 1930s, cannot be regarded as complete until the second half of the 1940s. This new technological substrategy was the driving force behind the subsequent American 'golden age' of the 1950s and 1960s.

The Great Depression, therefore, was not part of the widely accepted idea of a cyclical process of boom and bust in capitalism, but merely a hiatus between two technological substrategies. At best, 'countercyclical' policies such as lower interest rates and microeconomic reform (particularly of financial institutions) merely removed some of the supply obstacles to strategic revival. At worst, they led to institutional changes that were inappropriate and costly. Certainly they had no positive impact on the recovery process, which was only achieved through a renewal of strategic demand that elicited an appropriate supply-side response. It was strategic leadership that was really required, not supply-side reforms or even Keynesian static-demand policies, which merely have a very short-term effect on unemployment and absolutely no influence on the renewal of strategic demand (see Chapter 8).

The Roosevelt administration, despite its much trumpeted New Deal, failed to provide the strategic leadership that would have made a more proactive contribution to recovery. In the context of the 1930s, strategic leadership would have required Roosevelt to understand that the old technological substrategy had exhausted itself and that it was necessary to redirect the US economy from the domestic to the global market. This could have been done by listening not to neoclassical or even Keynesian experts but rather to the new strategists who were struggling to develop new markets overseas.

Neoclassical supply-side policies have no impact on recovery, and Keynesian static-demand policies have only a very shortrun impact. An artificial Keynesian increase in aggregate demand through increased public works will quickly ebb away and require further expenditure injections if these are not supported by a renewal of strategic demand and strategic confidence that depend not on government countercyclical expenditures but on the emergence of a new substrategy. It is for this totally unacknowledged reason that the recovery process during the 1930s fluctuated from year to year and was far from complete at the end of the decade. Indeed, in the late 1930s it appeared that the United States was slipping back into the depths of depression despite all its countercyclical policies, both orthodox and radical. Only when the new substrategy emerged in the late 1940s could the recovery process be said to be complete. *Only policies aimed at stimulating strategic demand and strategic confidence indirectly by encouraging the development of a new technological substrategy can have any longrun impact on the recovery process. Only strategic leadership can assist in this process.*

A new theory of global development

The above dynamic-strategy model for rich countries is part of a more general theory of global dynamics, called the **global strategic transition** (GST) theory, which encompasses poor countries. It is based on a systematic empirical study presented in my global history trilogy (1996–98) and developed formally in *Global Transition* (1999). The GST is a process by which an increasing number of societies are drawn into the vortex of dynamic interaction between the world's most economically advanced nations, which constitute the **global strategic core**. It is generated by the global unfolding of the prevailing industrial technological paradigm. This unfolding process is neither inevitable nor smooth, as can be seen in the fluctuating fortunes of the world economy throughout the history of civilisation. The twentieth century, for example, witnessed the Great Depression of the 1930s, the 'golden age' of the 1950s and 1960s and the slower, more uneven growth of its final 25 years, which was punctuated by strategic crises such as the one experienced by East Asia. And as the prosperity of the global strategic core has waxed and waned, so too has the economic development of the rest of the world (the **global strategic fringe**).

There have been four technological paradigms in human history – and as many GSTs – the pre-palaeolithic (scavenging), palaeolithic (hunting), neolithic (agriculture) and the modern (industrial). This can be seen in Figure 3.1. In each historical era the technological revolution began in a narrowly defined region – a dynamic hot spot – and thereafter spread throughout the rest of the known world. The palaeolithic revolution, which emerged in the rift valley of East Africa about 1.6 million years ago, took about 1.2 million years to spread around the globe; the neolithic revolution (Old World), which first appeared in the Jordan Valley about 11 000 years ago, took only 3000 years to extend to the rest of the known world; and the Industrial Revolution, which began in Britain about 200 years ago, should be complete sometime during the twenty-first century. Clearly the GST is accelerating with the emergence of each new technological paradigm. The sequence of GSTs has been transformed from a smouldering fire into a raging inferno.

Figure 3.1, which illustrates these technological paradigm shifts, is designed to show two things: the stepped profile of *potential* real GDP per capita at the global level made possible by each paradigm shift (continuous line); and the more gradual increase in *actual* real GDP per capita (broken line). As can be seen, potential living standards increase relatively steeply – becoming increasingly steep as the present is approached – but are then stationary for much longer periods of time; periods that diminish in length by geometric ratio. In contrast, actual living standards increase only gradually to the potential ceiling, tracing out a more wave-like development path. This catch-up process between actual and potential living standards

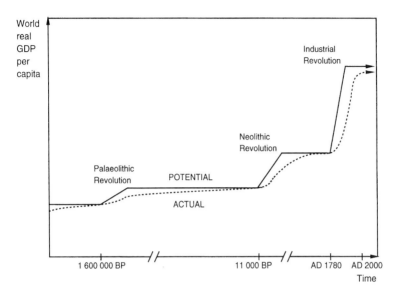

Figure 3.1   Global technological paradigm shifts
Source: Snooks, *The Dynamic Society* (London: Routledge, 1996), p. 403.

is an outcome of the GST, by which a highly competitive strategic core of rich countries gradually draws the strategic fringe of poor countries into its orbit.

This process of global economic development is an outcome of the limitless appetite of the strategic core for the underutilised natural and human resources of the strategic fringe. These resources are accessed through the pursuit of dynamic strategies that are specific to each technological paradigm – the family-multiplication strategy in the palaeolithic, conquest and commerce in the neolithic, and technological change in the modern. Each technological paradigm has been driven by its particular dynamic strategy. Once the current industrial paradigm has been fully exploited – once excess capacity has been finally wrung from the world's natural and human resources at this level of technology, and all its regions have been drawn into the strategic process – actual income will press persistently and urgently against the potential ceiling owing to the ever present struggle to survive and prosper. This is when the next paradigm shift will occur – unless it is derailed by inappropriate intervention.

While the wider historical context is essential for a full understanding of contemporary and future economic development, our main interest here is the modern GST, which has been in progress since the beginning of the British Industrial Revolution just two centuries ago. In relatively quick succession, Britain was followed by the Low Countries, France, Germany and the United States in the first half of the nineteenth century; by Sweden, Italy, Japan, Austria and Russia in the second half; by Canada, Australia, Argentina (temporarily) and Spain in the first half of the twentieth century; and by a raft of South European, East European and East Asian countries during the second half. While at the beginning of the twenty-first century no part of the globe remains untouched, many regions have yet to be drawn fully into the dynamic vortex of the global strategic core. These regions include much of Latin America, sub-Saharan Africa and parts of Southern and Southeast Asia.

Provided we do not derail the global unfolding process, even currently poor regions will pass through the GST some time during the course of the twenty-first century. Why? Because this has happened in human history on three earlier occasions, and because the fundamental driving force and dynamic mechanism underlying the current GST is no different today. What is particularly interesting is that earlier GSTs occurred without the 'assistance' of organisations such as the IMF and the World Bank or the army of economic experts who wish us to believe that they are indispensable to the achievement of economic development. In fact even the present GST had been under way for more than 150 years before these organisations and experts even existed. If anything, the GST has slowed since the middle of the twentieth century. As I show in *Global Transition* (1999), it is only through the intervention of these economic experts that the GST will be frustrated.

The modern GST is a dynamic process driven by an intense competition between a growing number of new entrants. Central to this dynamic is **global strategic demand**, which is the dynamic demand generated by the global unfolding of the technological paradigm. While most of this demand is met by societies within the global strategic core, some of it spills over to drive the economic development of poor countries in the strategic fringe. What attracts core countries to the fringe is the latter's stocks of relatively unused natural resources, cheap labour and their potential ability to supply raw materials and foods. Fringe countries most able to respond to changes in global strategic demand are those most quickly drawn into the GST. This strategic demand–response mechanism at the global level is orchestrated by rising prices (strategic inflation) that in turn provide the incentives for fringe countries to respond. Without strategic inflation there would be no supply response, no GST and no economic development. Of course nonstrategic inflation is deforming and must be eliminated by the pursuit of sensible monetary policy.

The unfolding industrial technological paradigm has passed through a number of distinct substrategies. The pioneering substrategy was pursued by Britain between the 1780s and 1830s in order to maintain its global supremacy following the exhaustion of its highly successful commerce strategy in the 1750s – a strategy that had created a global empire that was now at risk. This first-generation substrategy was based on the innovations of practical men and was undertaken through the establishment of small-scale enterprises that focused on a limited range of basic commodities such as cotton textiles, iron and steel, and simple engineering products. These enterprises began as family firms and small partnerships, largely self-financing, which gradually gave way to larger public companies drawing on wider sources of funding. Individual initiatives were transformed into social objectives through the process of **strategic imitation** whereby successful pioneers were imitated by growing numbers of followers. This type of early industrial development was well suited to the societal organisation of the nation-state that had emerged in Western Europe's pre-modern period in response to the former dynamic strategies of conquest and commerce.

The second technological substrategy was initiated by other nation-states in Western Europe between the 1830s and 1870s. Earlier experimentation with industrialisation on the Continent, particularly by France, had been disrupted by a continued fascination with conquest. But with the failure of Napoleon's conquest objectives, Western Europe as a whole turned its attention to the technological strategy. In order to compete with Britain in the continual struggle to survive and prosper, the leaders of France and Germany – and later Japan in the East – used tariff protection to imitate the British strategy and build state-of-the-art capital-intensive industries in engineering and chemicals. These new industries relied to a greater extent than the pioneering industries on scientific ideas and institutional finance. While the enterprises in this phase were more extensive and operated through a wider network of larger factories, they were accommodated within the existing nation-state structure.

The third technological substrategy began in North America in the 1890s and flourished during the following century. It had its origins in the determination of American industrialists and their political representatives to drive the Europeans from their large and growing domestic market and, later, to make inroads into the even larger world market. The United States was able to achieve its material objective by employing existing rather than new technological ideas on a scale that no other nation in the late nineteenth century could emulate. This was made possible by the strategic leadership provided by their governments, especially through the use of tariff protection until the United States was able to establish its new comparative advantage. Through large-scale investment in mass-production and mass-distribution techniques, the United States was able to exploit its giant domestic market by supplying goods at prices the Europeans were unable to match. The method was to employ a high degree of specialisation through assembly-line techniques in order to produce standardised products that could be distributed in bulk.

Once the domestic market had been fully exploited, by the mid 1920s, American entrepreneurs eventually turned their attention – following a strategic hiatus usually called the Great Depression – to world markets. After the Second World War this fourth substrategy was highly successful for the United States and other members of the growing global strategic core. It was a success enhanced by the extension of the mega-corporation – which can only emerge in a mega-state – producing a wide range of commodities and services. When they established branches in overseas markets these mega-corporations became known as multinational or transnational corporations. They are, in effect, agents of the technological strategies of the mega-state and they play an important role in the GST.

The fifth technological substrategy was developed by innovative nation-states at the end of the 'golden age' in an attempt to undermine the post-Second World War dominance of the US mega-state. It is particularly interesting that the societies pioneering this new strategic thrust were the nation-states that had failed in a mid-century attempt to meet growing American hegemony by developing mega-states of their own through conquest in Europe and Asia. In the late 1960s the reconstructed German and Japanese nation-states discovered that they could effectively compete against the United States in both the North American and the world markets by embracing the new microelectronic technology. If they were unable to transform themselves into mega-states at the expense of their immediate neighbours, perhaps they could economically undermine the foundations of the US mega-state. Through more efficient production and organisation, Germany and Japan were able to offer consumers greater variety and choice, even though this meant shorter production runs (only one-quarter that of the United States in the case of car production). They were able to combine old mass-production methods with the new microelectronic technology to make 'customised' consumer products of a higher quality. These more desirable commodities were in the categories of cars, household appliances, ceramics, textiles, consumer durables, computers and computer software. As consumers, who were tired of standardised products, responded to this greater choice with considerable enthusiasm, other nations in Europe and East Asia followed the German/Japanese lead. Even the United States in the 1980s was forced to compete with these new strategists on their own ground.

Finally, we come to the sixth technological substrategy of the modern era, which will dominate the global economy in the twenty-first century. With the conclusion of the Second World War it became clear to West European nation-states on both sides of the conflict that, by standing alone, not one of them could command the economic resources required to successfully compete, either militarily or economically, with the United States. It also became clear that the USSR was going to become a mega-state to rival the United States. Mega-status, therefore, was going to be essential for Western Europe, not only to defend the technological strategy it had given the world but also to engage in effective economic bargaining on a global scale, to exercise strategic control over a large and growing market, and to control a massive resource base.

The future will be determined by economic giants employing the latest microelectronic/biotechnological programmes. This is the real driving force behind the remarkable attempt to fashion Europe into a mega-state – remarkable because these societies have been engaged in a ferocious struggle against each other for more than a millennium. Such is the power of strategic demand. And we can expect the United States and the EU to be joined in their mega-club by China, once it throws off its communist chains, Russia, once it successfully achieves its transition, and possibly others (Japan and Southeast Asia) once the reality of the new substrategy becomes clear.

The main outcomes of the GST for the Third World since the middle of the twentieth century have been higher levels of real GDP per capita together with those changes in sociopolitical institutions that were required to pursue a dependent technological strategy. These new institutions include the rule of law, protection of private property, enforcement of contracts, a range of commercial rules and new political arrangements and social customs. Not included, as yet, are greater equity in the distribution of income, effective economic and political democracy, and 'human development' in terms of universal education, health and welfare. But these will be achieved in the next few generations as the GST unfolds.

Today there is a widespread demand in the West for the introduction of advanced forms of political democracy and income equity in the Third World. Some even claim a strong causal link between political democracy and economic growth. Nothing could be further from the truth. It is a view that demonstrates a complete misunderstanding of the nature of the dynamic process. As I show in my global history trilogy, high and sustained rates of economic growth in conquest and commerce societies were completely consistent with the most unequal distribution of political power and material living standards. While there is a high correlation between economic wealth and political power, the degree to which both are distributed in the population depends on the type of dynamic strategy adopted and the stage reached in the unfolding of that strategy. Even during the early stages of the modern technological paradigm, when the pioneering societies grew rapidly, wealth and power was limited to a small proportion of the population.

In Britain during the first half of the nineteenth century, for example, the political franchise was restricted to the wealthy landowning class and the new industrial upper-middle class. These were the old strategists who had derived their wealth from an earlier age of commerce and had invested it in land, together with the new strategists who had invested in the capital assets required by the new British technological strategy. Both groups were locked in a **strategic struggle** to gain control over Britain's dynamic strategy and over the distribution of its income. Once the new strategists gained the upper hand, industrialisation proceeded rapidly, drawing into its vortex the working classes, who invested in the human capital required by Britain's dynamic strategy and consequently shared in its material and political returns.

The same process will occur in Third World countries. As the GST progresses and, consequently, as the new technological strategy of a Third World country unfolds, the proportion of the population inducted into the strategic group will increase. This will lead to a strategic struggle between the ruling elite (who are rent-seeking anti-strategists rather than profit-seeking old strategists as in Britain) and the emerging new strategists. As the wealth and numbers of the new strategists increase, the old ruling elite will be forced either to share political power or to leave political office completely. At first, wealth and power will be controlled by a small group of strategists but, as their economic success increases and their technological sub-strategy continues to unfold, an ever larger proportion of the population will be drawn into the strategic group to contribute to the success of the dominant strategy and share in the economic and political returns.

There are no short cuts to democracy, as much as we may wish otherwise. If advanced forms of democracy are imposed on poor countries by external powers, the dynamic process in the Third World will be disrupted, even derailed. Owing to the threat that this conclusion poses to the self-interest of the 'development industry' – consisting of politicians, bureaucrats and intellectuals – I have no doubt that it will be attacked savagely. But experience will show that the strategic demand–response mechanism cannot be disrupted without causing crisis.

The world today

Is there really an 'Asian meltdown'? Will this spill over into a global crisis, as many are now suggesting? Is the financial crisis really at the centre of these global problems? Will the Third World ever catch up economically and politically? The answers to these questions, which are at the forefront of many minds at the beginning of the new millennium, can be found in the dynamic-strategy model outlined above.

Is there really an 'Asian meltdown'?

The problems that Japan, the largest economy in the region and the second largest in the world, experienced in the 1990s were a natural outcome of the exhaustion of the technological substrategy it pursued so successfully for two generations after the Second World War. During that time the world marvelled at the extremely rapid and sustained rates of economic growth achieved by Japan. It was regarded enviously by the West as an economic 'miracle'. There was no talk then about 'crony capitalism' or unworkable labour and capital markets. Quite the reverse. At that time many star-struck observers suggested that other Asian and even Western countries should imitate the institutional structure of Japan. Only now that Japan is experiencing an embarrassing economic decline are the same observers condemning the very institutions and practices that they once extravagantly praised.

Japan's problems in the early 1990s heralded a wider slow-down and 'crisis' in East Asia in the later part of the decade. Those East Asian countries – such as South Korea, Thailand and Indonesia – that did adopt aspects of the much-vaunted Japanese model have also undergone the same process of strategic exhaustion. All this, despite the extravagant reaction of the doomsayers, is quite normal. As my dynamic-strategy model predicts, these countries are merely experiencing the hiatus that always separates successful technological substrategies. Provided these countries do not panic and give way to pressure from the West to implement deforming neoliberal policies, they will develop new substrategies that will lead to the resumption of rapid economic growth and eventually to the achievement of liberty.

The financial problems currently being experienced in these East Asian economies are an outcome of the exhaustion of strategic opportunities. Financial practices that appear in retrospect unsound, even excessively corrupt, emerged largely in the exhaustion phase of the former technological substrategy. These practices were particularly associated with growing speculative and rent-seeking activities as strategic (profit-seeking) opportunities declined. Once strategic demand and strategic confidence finally collapsed in these countries, their speculative booms were no longer sustainable. In turn this led to a collapse in the confidence of international speculators in East Asian assets, real and financial (including currencies) and, hence, to a decline in their prices on stock exchanges around the world.

According to the dynamic-strategy model, all this will be reversed once new technological substrategies are developed by these East Asia countries. In other words their institutions and practices should not be 'reformed' in the light of deforming neoliberal ideas as they will respond appropriately to the renewal of strategic demand. There is just no way that the requirements of the new technological substrategy can be determined in advance of this revival. In addition to being unnecessarily costly, neoliberal institutional 'reforms' may even act as a barrier to strategic revival. Similarly, as new strategic opportunities emerge the attractiveness of rent-seeking, speculation and corruption will decline. This should happen in the next few years, provided neoliberal policies of deflation and 'structural adjustment' are not forced on them by the IMF and the World Bank. *There is, in other words, no such thing as an 'Asian meltdown'.* We should not succumb to the pessimism of the financial doomsayers who tell us, without employing a general dynamic model, that 'East Asia's recovery from crisis could take decades'.

Will there be a spill-over from Asia to the rest of world?

The short answer to the above question is no, not in the present circumstances. Countries in other parts of the world at different stages of their own technological substrategies will merely alter their economic programmes to minimise the disruption emanating from East Asia. This is what the world always does in such circumstances, which emerge at regular intervals. Remember also that East Asian countries are responding to strategic demand generated by the global strategic core and, with the exception of Japan, they are not driving it. As core countries largely interact with each other rather than with the strategic fringe, we should not expect the impact of these temporary problems in East Asia to be very significant as far as the rest of the world is concerned.

Other regional problems, such as those in Russia or Brazil, certainly add to the world's overall difficulties, but once again these more random events are not unusual. Russia collapsed during and after the First World War without catastrophic consequences for the rest of the world; and China experienced similar problems during and after the Second World War, and again in the 1960s. In addition the global economy today is in a better position to handle this type of problem than it was in the 1920s. There is just no logical reason to expect that today's normal strategic problems will create a crisis in the rest of the world, unless, that is, we insist on employing neoliberal policies.

Do the current financial problems constitute a global crisis?

Once again the short answer is no. These problems are merely the outcome of the normal exhaustion of technological substrategies in East Asia. Financial issues, therefore, should not be the focus of remedial action. Unsound institutions should be allowed to go to the wall. This will help shake out the speculators and rent-seekers and hasten the emergence of a new substrategy. Economic recovery will only follow a strategic revival, which will generate a renewal of strategic demand and strategic confidence. This will not only rejuvenate the real economy, it will also sort out remaining institutional problems in the finance and labour sectors. *Financial 'reforms' will not of themselves lead to economic recovery.*

What governments in East Asia should be providing is strategic leadership rather than spending vast sums on financial reconstruction, as Western experts are currently suggesting. As suggested earlier, by acting before the emergence of a new substrategy, much money will be wasted and the process of strategic revitalisation will be delayed. Why? Because the static models of neoclassical economics cannot predict the changing strategic requirements of a dynamic world. Strategic leadership, on the other hand, involves the provision of financial encouragement to pioneering strategists, together with the infrastructure they require to launch their new substrategy.

While Keynesian static-demand policies will not assist this strategic renewal, they may help to keep the economy afloat in the very shortrun until it occurs. Neoliberal policies will not help at all; indeed, by virtue of their deflationary nature, they will only make the economic situation worse. Policies of financial 'reform' should be seen for what they are – attempts to salvage the interests of speculators and financiers, rather than to promote the cause of the strategists who drive the dynamics of human society.

Will democracy lead to a revival of growth?

As suggested earlier, the short answer is an emphatic no. Economic growth is an outcome of the interaction between strategic demand and the strategic instruments, whereas the degree of democratisation is an outcome of the strategic struggle. Rapid and sustained economic growth can be achieved with or without democracy, and democracy can preside over rapid or negative economic growth. Any attempt by the mega-states or their agents, the IMF and the World Bank, to impose advanced systems of democracy on Third World countries will either be subverted if outside controls are ineffective (the most likely outcome) or will derail the fledgling development process if outside controls are binding (an outside possibility).

Liberty will emerge only as a growing proportion of the population is drawn into the strategic process. Only as the new strategists gain economic power – an outcome of a successful dynamic process – will they be able to wrest political control over the sources of their wealth from the old ruling elite. And only as strategic demand expands to include the services of most of the population will these countries adopt systems of universal democracy similar to those in the West. Progress and liberty are inextricably bound together, but not in the way envisaged by neoliberals.

Will the Third World ever develop?

For a change the short answer is yes, provided that those global agents of neoliberalism, the IMF and the World Bank, do not continue to disrupt the GST through their destructive 'structural adjustment' programmes. As both human history and my global strategic-transition model show, the process of global development will, over the next few generations, draw most of the remaining regions of the Third World into the GST. This is a self-starting and self-sustaining process that has occurred successfully on all three former occasions in human history. The GST model presented in my recent book, *Global Transition* (1999), which is firmly based on historical experience, shows why this is so. Significantly, these earlier global transitions were achieved without the intervention of economic experts and development agencies. Intellectuals and their fellow-travellers do more damage by interfering out of ignorance than by doing nothing at all. Perhaps they should be paid to retrain for more useful employment. It would certainly be far less costly for the world than having them interfere in matters they are not equipped to handle.

Conclusions

It is absolutely essential that we understand the global dynamic process before attempting to interfere with it. Orthodox economic experts have demonstrated clearly over the past half century that they are not qualified to understand this process and that their policies are undermining its long-term viability. Their discipline, which is really a branch of production engineering, is only useful for examining static microeconomic relationships. It is hardly surprising, therefore, that they focus on issues of financial stability rather than real dynamic change. Only by developing realistic dynamic models can we hope to understand what is really happening globally and thereby avoid bringing progress and liberty to an end.

4
The Universal Role of Strategic Leadership

Throughout the history of human society a close relationship has existed between the dynamic strategists and their leaders. It is a relationship essential to the prosperity of nations and civilisations. But it is a relationship that has broken down during the last quarter of the twentieth century. By the 1980s, governments of the Western world had transformed themselves from strategic leaders into crisis makers, and by the end of the century many had emerged triumphant over the strategists. The crisis makers have become the antistrategists of the developed world. Yet their triumph is hollow. They now preside over a fibrillating world – a world destined for collapse unless the role of strategic leadership is rediscovered.

The essential function of strategic leadership

Strategic leadership is essential to the survival and prosperity of human society. It was, as already noted, the primary reason for the emergence of government at the dawn of human civilisation and for its extension and maintenance ever since. The nature of strategic leadership will become clearer when we review the way it has worked throughout human history. Basically it involves facilitating the objectives of society's dynamic strategists. This is achieved by coordinating the efforts of strategists, directly through government directives and incentives, and indirectly through cultural institutions such as religion, ideology and the arts. In particular the state provides basic infrastructure that is beyond the financial resources of individuals and corporations, it negotiates political and economic deals with other societies, it protects the dynamic strategy at home and abroad, it encourages the emergence of new strategies during recessions/depressions and it provides basic facilities for the education, training and research required to nourish the modern technological strategy. This is a proactive rather than a passive role, and it is provided by representatives of the strategists for the benefit of the strategists. To achieve this, successful strategic leaders listen carefully to what the strategists think they require in order to achieve their objectives and respond objectively to what they hear.

It is important to realise that the strategists do not necessarily encompass the entire population of a society. They include only those individuals who invest, in either physical or human capital terms, in the dominant dynamic strategy. The proportion of the population that can be classified among the strategists has varied throughout human history, not in a linear but in a circular way. In palaeolithic society, almost all adult members were involved in the family-multiplication strategy, with the result that the proportion of the population in the strategist category approached 100 per cent. Hence tribal leaders needed to take into consideration the aspirations of all adults. By contrast, in neolithic society only a small proportion of the population was actively involved in the strategic pursuit, owing to the economic monopoly of the ruling elite. This proportion ranged from less than 1 per cent in societies based on dependent agriculture (lords and slaves/serfs) to about one-quarter in mercantile societies. Only in advanced technological societies has the strategists/population ratio once more approached that of hunter–gatherer societies. The forces underlying these sociopolitical changes are examined in the rest of this chapter.

Strategic Leadership in History

The style of strategic leadership is determined by the prevailing dynamic strategy and by the stage reached in its unfolding process. As shown in *The Dynamic Society* (1996), there have been four different types of human society over the past two million years: the nomadic society, the conquest society, the commerce society and the technological society. The dynamic strategies that shape these different societies are an outcome of the prevailing technological era. The family-multiplication strategy of procreation and migration that underlay the nomadic society was the dominant dynamic strategy of the palaeolithic technological paradigm (2 million years to 11 000 years ago); conquest and commerce were the dominant strategies of the neolithic technological paradigm of agricultural societies (11 000 years ago to the mid-eighteenth century); and technological change is the dominant dynamic strategy of the modern industrial technological paradigm (mid-eighteenth century to the present).

Palaeolithic society

In the palaeolithic technological era, hunter–gatherers struggled to survive and prosper by increasing family size in order to bring more land resources under family control, thereby maximising the exploitation of animal and plant species. Sometimes this involved dispossessing and destroying less advanced humanoid species, such as Neanderthal man in Europe, and sometimes taking up virgin territory, such as Australia some 60 000 (or more) years ago and North America at least 15 000 years ago. In this way modern man circled the globe. But in order to achieve their material objectives the hunter–gatherers looked to family and tribal heads to provide strategic leadership.

An important aspect of this leadership was the wisdom that came with experience. Accordingly young men looked to family and tribal elders to provide the guidance needed in this technologically primitive world in order to survive and prosper. The relationship between leaders and other strategists in the family/tribe was close. Tribal leaders did not misunderstand their role as strategic leaders, because it led quickly to failure and the death not only of the strategists but also of the confused leader.

The success of the relationship between strategists and their leaders in palaeolithic society can be seen in the survival of Aboriginal society in Australia for more than 60 000 years before it was destroyed by Britain, the pioneering technological society. In contrast the technological society in Australia stands at the crossroads, as it does throughout the Western world, after little more than two centuries. Aboriginal society never lost sight of the role of strategic leadership as modern society has in the past few decades.

Neolithic society

The neolithic world was populated by a large number of highly competitive societies, all struggling to survive and prosper through the pursuit of either the conquest or the commerce strategy. While conquest was the normal dynamic strategy in this era, a favoured few societies were able to prosper by following the less exacting strategy of commerce. The very different requirements of these two strategies generated distinctly different societies in terms not only of their economic and political structures, but also of their social and cultural characteristics. As I show in *The Ephemeral Civilization* (1997), conquest societies followed a darker, wilder spirit, whereas commerce societies pursued the beauty of order and reason. To illustrate the different leader/ strategist relationship in these entirely different societies, I will briefly outline the rise and fall of the Roman conquest society (800 BC–AD 476) and the medieval Venetian commerce society (AD 810–1797).

Rome

Considerable misunderstanding exists about the nature of the conquest society. Instead of viewing systematic warfare as an integral part of the ancient economy, most treat it as an irrational and entirely negative activity. In reality, conquest was the dominant sector of the ancient economy, and it fashioned the central institutions around which all other institutions revolved. War was the main means by which survival and prosperity were achieved in the pre-modern world. Rome is the best documented case of this type of society.

How did the Roman dynamic work? The conquest strategy was driven by a small group of enterprising decision makers, or dynamic strategists, who were determined to survive in the highly competitive Mediterranean world and, having survived, maximise their material advantage. On their evaluation – determined by an intuitive benefit–cost approach – the best way of achieving this in a Mediterranean crowded out by aggressive commercial societies (the Greeks, Carthaginians and Etruscans) was through conquest. The resulting conquest strategy, which Rome pursued relentlessly for a millennium, consisted of a number of substrategies: tribal defence, 800–509 BC; break-out from the Tiber Valley to the coastal regions, 509–340 BC; conquest of all Italy, 340–264 BC; taking the strategy overseas (Punic Wars), 264–201 BC; turning to the east, 201–146 BC; expanding on all fronts, 146 BC–AD 180; and defending an exhausted strategy, AD 180–476. The rise and fall of the Roman conquest strategy had taken almost 1300 years to complete – our own technological strategy has been in progress for only a fraction of that time.

While Rome was originally led by tribal kings elected from among a small warrior elite, its main rise and fall took place under the Republic (509–43 BC) and the Principate (43 BC–AD 476). In the Republic of Rome the dynamic strategists were the senators, a land-owning, warrior aristocracy that grew in number from 300 to 900 over these five centuries. They were the leading members of the elite families of Rome, who took the major share of the profits of conquest and translated them into a steady stream of income through the acquisition of land (like purchasing gilt-edged securities today). This elite was supported and supplemented by the equestrian class (*equites*), who were engaged in trade, business, tax farming, supplying war materials and financing the political campaigns of the senators (for example, Julius Caesar). Clearly the *equites* had a vested interest in supporting the conquest aims of the senatorial class.

Both the state and the elite that it represented invested in the conquest strategy in the expectation of generating supernormal profits. The Republican state invested in military expeditions, military transport and communication networks, and in an imperial bureaucracy. It did this to facilitate the objectives of the leading families of Rome, because a conquest/imperial infrastructure could not be provided by individual families, particularly when Roman armies began operating outside Italy. Nevertheless, the warrior elite invested as heavily as their resources would allow in military and imperial skills, fame as a warrior, lobbying to attain military command and high political office, and even in military campaigns.

The return on this conquest investment was high, with the Roman state extracting plunder and taxation from the conquered provinces, and the strategists grabbing booty from military campaigns and high profits from imperial office. Even the common people supported the conquest strategy because they too had much to gain both as soldiers and citizens: as soldiers they shared in the spoils of war, which in some cases transformed their lives (like winning the lottery today); and as citizens they lived tax free and enjoyed subsidised consumption of necessities and of entertainment (as at the Colosseum from AD 80).

The Roman Senate was, in effect, a corporation with a form of limited liability and institutional longevity, as the risks were shared by the leading families of Rome and were underwritten by the larger, business oriented, equestrian class. Not surprisingly, therefore, the Republican Senate provided effective strategic leadership. As it directly represented the elite military/landowning class, it never lost sight of the strategy of Rome nor of its role in leading that strategy.

Why then did control of Rome's conquest strategy pass from the Senate to an autocrat after 30 BC? Essentially because of the changing requirements – the changing strategic demand – of the conquest strategy. As the Roman dynamic strategy unfolded the very scale of the conquest expeditions, which increased in proportion to the length of the Empire's frontier (geometrically rather than arithmetically), made it necessary to place immense power for prolonged periods in the hands of a few great military men such as Pompey the Great and Julius Caesar. Pompey was given greater power than former generals of the Republic in order to clear pirates from the eastern Mediterranean, and Caesar was given command over a large army for a decade in order to conquer Gaul. As these great military commanders were faced in Rome by men merely trained and experienced in law, politics and administration – men who did not command the respect of professional armies – there was little to stop them when they demanded absolute power over the conquest strategy and, hence, over Rome.

It was the unfolding conquest strategy, therefore, that led to the civil wars of the late Republic (the first century BC). Those wars were an acting out of the strategic struggle between the Senate and its great generals – a struggle between Sulla and Marius, Pompey and Caesar, Brutus/Cassius and Octavius/Anthony and, finally, between Octavius (then called Octavian and later Augustus) and Anthony/ Cleopatra. If Rome was to continue to expand and grow richer there could be but one outcome of these civil wars – the transformation of the Republic into an autocracy by the victorious general. By the beginning of the first century BC the conquest strategy had reached the stage beyond which it could continue to unfold only if new campaigns could be conducted on a massive and sustained scale, which was beyond the scope of the Republican Senate. Only a highly centralised system could mobilise the resources required. This solution finally emerged towards the end of the first century BC.

By 30 BC, control of Rome's conquest strategy was firmly in the hands of an autocrat, Emperor Augustus, who invited the surviving ruling families (which he had ruthlessly purged) to participate, in effect, as non-voting shareholders. In this way Augustus eliminated the former counterproductive competition between members of the aristocracy. As head of the Roman army, the emperor became the supreme dynamic strategist and, hence, a god worshipped by all strategists. In the Republic, where strategic leadership was shared equally among members of the warrior elite, their pantheon of gods was external to Roman society.

Yet in one essential matter there was continuity. Strategic leaders in Rome, both before and after the civil wars, used cultural institutions such as religion, the arts and the games, to help reinforce the conquest strategy in their society. These cultural activities were essential because they involved all the population, even nonstrategists (merchants, businessmen, workers) in Rome's conquest strategy. And as I show in *The Ephemeral Civilization* (1997), these cultural institutions embodied and carried forward the spirit of conquest. Only when the conquest strategy had been exhausted, around AD 180, were the Roman gods of war replaced by the Christian god.

Also, until the Roman dynamic strategy had been exhausted the relationship between leader and strategist was both close and mutually profitable. The Romans never forgot the essential role of strategic leadership and never required the services of economic experts. Rome declined not because its strategists and strategic leaders failed, but because they were remarkably successful in exploiting their dynamic strategy to the full. Will we be able to say the same?

Venice

Commerce societies existed in the neolithic era just beyond the reach, in both space and time, of great conquest empires. There was no scope for coexistence as commerce societies were irresistible to conquest predators. As history shows, Assyria harried Phoenicia, Rome crushed Carthage, Macedonia overwhelmed the Greeks and finally swept away the Phoenicians, and the Napoleonic empire extinguished the Republic of Venice. Yet while they flourished these commerce societies, which sought the beauty of order and reason rather than the chaos of a darker imagination, made a contribution to the culture of human civilisation that was not surpassed until the emergence of the technological strategy of the modern era. To illustrate the role of strategic leadership in the commerce society, I will focus on the rise and fall of medieval Venice.

Just as the commerce strategy adopted by the city-states of ancient Greece led to a golden age of cultural and political attainment in the classical world, the same strategy employed by the north Italian city-states of the medieval and early-modern world led to the classical revival known as the Renaissance. This cultural flowering was not a coincidence. In both cases it was an outcome of strategic demand generated by the economic dynamic of commerce. Venice played an important role in these developments because, for the six centuries following the First Crusade of 1095, it was the leading commerce society in Europe. And as its commerce strategy unfolded, Venetian sociopolitical institutions flourished under the driving influence of strategic demand.

Venice is the most successful example of a 'pure' commerce society. Because they had no land resources, the Venetians were engaged in trade right from the very beginning – from the late sixth century AD, when Roman families on the mainland were forced into the lagoons at the head of the Adriatic Sea by the invading Lombards. To survive, these peoples had to trade the sea resources of salt and fish for grain and other foods from the mainland. But the Venetians were able to turn their poverty of resources into a major asset because they commanded the gateway to trade between Europe and the Orient.

As the inhabitants of the lagoons grew in number and maritime power, they were able to transform their primitive trading activities into a commerce strategy that generated supernormal profits owing to their monopoly over key trading routes. This was achieved in three distinct stages. The first of these occupied the four centuries prior to the First Crusade, when Venetian boatmen traded goods throughout the lagoons and along the rivers of northern Italy. As their trade expanded the Venetians carried – in addition to their harvest of the seas – spices, silks, incense and slaves brought to Venice by Greek traders from the Levant. The second stage in Venice's commerce strategy involved extending its trading control throughout the Adriatic by clearing the region of pirates and rival fleets operating from the mainland of Italy and Dalmatia (modern Yugoslavia). This was accomplished during the tenth and eleventh centuries and the Adriatic became the Venetian 'lake', giving access to the surrounding lands as well as to key trading routes.

Stage three involved a break-out from the Adriatic into the rest of the Mediterranean. This was achieved by negotiating trading privileges in the Byzantine Empire in 1082, and by exploiting trading opportunities in the Levant made possible by the Crusades, which began in 1095. The most remarkable of the Crusades was the Fourth in 1202–4, which was skilfully diverted by Venice in order to do what the Infidel had failed to do, namely to sack the Christian city of Constantinople and dismember the Byzantine Empire. In the process Venice acquired three-eighths of the entire empire. In the ancient world one had to be wary of Greeks bearing gifts, but in the medieval world it was necessary to defend oneself against Venetians on holy business. With this acquisition of trading posts and colonies throughout Romania (the old Byzantine Empire) the Republic was able to dominate Mediterranean trade between Europe and the Levant. For a further century Venetian commerce flourished.

But by the mid-fourteenth century Venice's commerce strategy was approaching exhaustion owing to the advance of Muslim forces in the east and of Aragon's and, later, Spain's forces in the west. Declining commercial opportunities led Venice into conflict with its main rival, Genoa, in the 1350s and again in the 1370s, and also to experiments with the new dynamic strategy of conquest in northern Italy during the fifteenth century. While Venice was able to defeat Genoa at sea, the conquest experiment on land almost ended in disaster in the early sixteenth century when a union of all Europe turned against the predatory Venice. This ended its dreams of plunder. With commerce exhausted and conquest in ruins, Venice had no strategic future. From 1529, therefore, the Republic (like Rome after 180 BC) merely attempted to defend its past achievements through diplomacy, first with Europe in the west and then, after 1718, with the Ottoman Empire in the east. But it was only a matter of time before the former glorious republic was swept away. The end finally came in 1797 at the hands of the last great Mediterranean conqueror, Napoleon Bonaparte.

At the time of its independence from the Byzantine Empire around AD 1000, the Venetian commune consisted of about sixty small communities, or parishes, which, subject to the approval and supervision of the Doge, elected their own chiefs (*capi di contrada*) from the wealthy local merchant families. A *capo* was responsible for raising taxes, organising naval service and undertaking local policy duties. The focus of this network of parishes was the central market-place, the Rialto, where the main inter-parish and international commerce was conducted. Later it became the centre of east–west trade between the Levant and the North Sea.

It is significant that the Rialto is connected by a short canal to the Piazza San Marco and the Piazzetta – the central community squares in Venice – adjoining the Ducal Palace (residence of the Doge) and the church of San Marco (not the cathedral of Venice but the splendid private chapel of the strategic leader). In turn the Piazzetta provides access to the Bacino di San Marco, where the larger ships moored. The close proximity of Venice's main dock, the Rialto, the Ducal Palace, and the Doge's church symbolises the equally close relationship between the commerce strategy and the political and cultural institutions of the Republic. Venice had no doubt about the central role of strategic leadership.

Just as local officials were elected by parish assemblies, so the Doge, in the beginning, was elected for life by acclamation of the General Assembly, consisting of all the male inhabitants of the lagoons. In the tenth and eleventh centuries the Doge theoretically derived his authority from the entire community, but in reality his election was controlled by the leading merchant families. And before the revolution of 1026, when the ruling Orseolo dynasty was over-thrown by the leading merchant nobles, the Doge was in effect a monarch for life with unlimited powers. In the early centuries following independence, therefore, Venice was a dukedom rather than a commune. After the revolution, however, the Doge's powers were constrained by a council of elected merchant aristocrats. In this way the Venetian nobility – who built their grand houses around the Piazza San Marco to be near the seat of government, where the direction of the commerce strategy was decided – moved a step closer to a merchant oligarchy.

With the growing wealth and power of the leading noble families after the Venetian break-out into the Mediterranean in the late eleventh century, this elite found it profitable to take control of the commerce strategy then still largely in the hands of the Doge. For most of the twelfth century the Michiel family had occupied the Ducal Palace and had regularly ignored the advice of its merchant councils. The outcome was a breakdown in the essential relationship between its strategists and the leadership. The ensuing reaction was predictable.

Following a disastrous punitive expedition against the Byzantine emperor led by the Doge in 1172, which returned with nothing but a decimating pestilence, the leading merchants deposed and assassinated Doge Vitalle II Michiel. In future the Doge would be elected directly from the ranks of the leading merchants and would never again be permitted to reject the advice of his peers. By this act Venice became a merchant oligarchy with a republican form of government, as required by a rapidly expanding commerce society. The essential relationship between leader and strategist was restored and effective strategic leadership was reintroduced. Without this revolution, Venetian society would have soon stagnated and collapsed.

The determination of the merchant nobility to retain control of Venice's dynamic strategy is also reflected in its refusal to hand over administration of the commerce strategy to a central bureaucracy. Government strategic policy was the responsibility of small committees of three to six unpaid nobles, elected by the Great Council and supervised by the governing council. In this way the strategists of Venice avoided the modern problem of experts hijacking the dynamic strategy. The Venetian Republic was to remain a benefit society for mercantile interests.

While the commerce strategy was unfolding, Venice's merchant oligarchy provided a flexible form of government that admitted wealthy merchants into the highest ruling councils. Only once the commerce strategy had been exhausted, by the mid-fourteenth century, did the existing ruling elite attempt to perpetuate their power and wealth by blocking new aspirants to the Great Council, which represented some 200 families, with just 30 of these exercising effective power. On turning from commerce to conquest during the fifteenth century, the city-state was transformed into an imperial state with captured territories on the mainland of Italy and Dalmatia. And as this new strategy unfolded, the degree of democratisation achieved earlier was reversed. In particular the General Assembly was abolished, the 'commune' of Venice was dissolved, and the Great Council of some 2500 members ceded its power to the 300-strong Senate. Even the Senate was effectively controlled by the governing council, or *Signoria*, which included merely the Doge and the nine leading members of the Senate steering committee. This concentration of political power and leadership is typical of a conquest society.

After the failure of the Venetian conquest strategy the political system was deserted by its bold, energetic, ambitious and imaginative citizens and left in the hands of those seekers after empty status. Strategic leadership in Venice withered once its dynamic strategies had been exhausted, because a static society has no need of direction. The end was only a matter of time, and when it came the once glorious republic gave up without a struggle. In the end there was nothing worth fighting over.

Technological society

The ancients accepted the reality of the eternal recurrence. Accepted that even the greatest civilisations would eventually stagnate, collapse and phoenix-like, rise anew. The ruins of past civilisations were there for all to see. They did not even consider the possibility of breaking out of this endlessly repetitive pattern, because in the neolithic era there was no material incentive to do so. The fall of great conquest and commerce societies such as Rome and Venice was inevitable. This is why we must consider the industrial technological society as an entirely new entity.

Since the mid-eighteenth century, material incentives have favoured the pursuit of the technological strategy. This dynamic strategy has enabled modern society to escape from the eternal recurrence and, so far, to achieve sustained material progress. The dynamic pathway of the modern world is linear (but wave-like) rather than circular (and wave-like). Political institutions, therefore, no longer reemerge from the ashes in familiar forms, but develop in entirely new ways.

But this continuous linear development must not be thought of as inevitable. If we continue to enforce self-destructive neoliberal policies, modern society will return to the ancient dynamic process of eternal recurrence. To show how the West emerged from this ancient dynamic pattern I will focus briefly on the first nation-state to successfully adopt the technological strategy (Britain), and on the first mega-state to take it to a logical conclusion (the United States). If we fail to learn from the past we will be condemned to relive it.

Britain

The rise of Western civilisations cannot be attributed to any single state. It was an outcome of the response of many societies throughout the world to a highly competitive physical and human environment that gradually exhausted the neolithic technological paradigm of the pre-modern world. The last phase of this process took the form of an intense interaction between the kingdoms of Western Europe and between these and their immediate neighbours.

For some seven centuries England/Britain struggled desperately with its neighbours for survival in the pressure-cooker circumstances of Western Europe. England was so transformed by this struggle that early in the seventeenth century it suddenly broke out of its immediate environment into all parts of the world to form the largest, most global empire the world has ever known. Yet this great empire was considerably more ephemeral than those of the ancient world. Within just three centuries the British Empire rose, flourished, basked in its own glory for a brief season, and then fell. While the ancients would have been impressed by the global scope of the British achievement, they would have been astounded not so much by the rapidity of its fall as by the unique fact that after the dust had settled, Britain still existed, with a viable society and a standard of living higher than that in the greatest days of empire. And still growing rapidly. For the first time in history a great empire had been able to downsize to its homeland without collapsing. Britain was able to succeed where Rome, Venice and all the rest had failed – because it was able to adopt the technological strategy.

Britain's development pathway between 1000 and 2000 AD took the form of three great linear waves, each of which was up to 300 years in duration. These 'great waves', which surged forward during the periods 1000–1300, 1480–1750, and the 1760s–2000, were generated by three very different dynamic strategies – conquest, commerce and technological change. Each of these dynamic strategies was composed of a series of substrategies that generated long waves of about 50 years. With the exhaustion of each dynamic strategy, Britain was fortunate enough to be able to replace it – albeit after a hiatus during which stagnation or decline was experienced – with an entirely new one. In this way Britain managed to avoid the collapse that had occurred in all ancient societies. Yet, as I show in the global history trilogy, this was due more to fortunate timing than to superior strategic skills.

The institutional vehicle for the conquest society in Western Europe was the nation-state, strategically directed by a hereditary monarchy. In this political system, England's dynamic strategists were the king and his great magnates, who struggled against each other for control of the conquest strategy and for all the rewards that it brought. The most famous of these struggles took place between the Angevin king called John (1199–1216) and his barons in the early thirteenth century, and between John's son, Henry III (1216–72), and his barons, led by Simon de Montfort. The first of these struggles was largely an outcome of John's incompetent strategic leadership, which dramatically reduced, rather than increased, the wealth and income of his barons (or strategists). Despite the heavy, regular land taxes imposed by John to pay for his wars, the English king not only failed to capture additional territory in Europe, but actually lost all that he and his barons had previously held. It was this failure of strategic leadership that led the long-suffering barons to rebel and force their king to sign Magna Carta in 1215.

The great charter was not about human rights, as some might suppose, but about the material rights of a tiny fraction of the population. This ruling elite, both lay and ecclesiastical, insisted that the function of government was to facilitate the objectives of all those participating in the conquest strategy. It was a clear warning to any king who lacked the desire or ability to provide strategic leadership that he would be removed. Demonstration of this declaration was not long in coming. The expensive failure of Henry III's conquest strategy in Europe provoked a struggle with his barons, led by Simon de Montfort, between 1258 and 1265. Although Henry eventually eliminated the rebellious and briefly successful de Montfort, he was forced to accept the role of strategic leadership – to facilitate the objectives of the strategists.

The English king financed the conquest – an expensive and risky undertaking – by imposing taxes on the surplus generated by agriculture and increasingly on the growing profits of commerce. But to tax these growing commercial interests (largely in the production and exportation of raw wool), the king found it necessary to gain their formal approval by inviting their representatives to attend parliament at Westminster. From 1258 these included two 'knights' (growers of wool) from each shire, and in 1265 a further two burgesses (wool merchants) from each of the main boroughs. Parliament met in two chambers, the Commons (knights and burgesses) and the Lords (great magnates, both lay and ecclesiastical).

From the mid-thirteenth century, therefore, the English monarch was only able to raise the funds required to finance the conquest strategy by taxing and consulting the emerging commercial interests. While the new political institution of Parliament (a place for 'speaking') was developed initially to serve the failing conquest strategy, in the late fourteenth and early fifteenth centuries it became the stage for a desperate struggle between the aristocratic supporters of the old conquest strategy on the one hand, and the middle-class supporters of the new commerce strategy on the other. This struggle was eventually resolved, but only through civil war, in favour of the supporters of commerce.

The major focus of the commerce society is the city. Owing to the extraordinary profits generated by the commerce strategy through its monopoly access to resources, commodities and markets, its metropolis is able to achieve a size unimagined by neolithic societies relying solely on agriculture. People are attracted to these centres of commerce by the spectacular growth of real income and wealth to be earned in urban trade, finance and manufacturing. And as the commerce strategy unfolds, the metropolis becomes the centre of an overseas empire.

Within this institutional framework, in the period 1500–1700 a great struggle took place in England between the supporters of the competing dynamic strategies of conquest and commerce. The outcome had critical implications for the nature of the political and economic system not only of England but also of Europe and the world. Had the old feudal aristocracy won this struggle, then England, like France and Spain, would have turned once more to the conquest strategy, and the Industrial Revolution would have been delayed at great cost in terms of human life, prosperity and liberty.

As conquest declined and commerce increased during the fifteenth century, the wealth of the new mercantile middle class grew in relation to that of the old warrior aristocracy. Hence when the Tudor dynasty first came to power in 1485, it was to the new men of commerce rather than the old men of conquest that they turned for support. Henry VII, who understood that survival meant embracing the new strategists, was the first English monarch to make the transition of leadership from a conquest to a commerce strategy. In a highly competitive world, the decision to lead the commerce strategy in England meant leading it in Western Europe. Elizabeth I embraced this role. Her war against Spain was not a war of conquest but a war in defence of the commerce strategy both at sea and on the continent of Europe. It was a war in support of the Netherlands – that other pioneering commerce society in Western Europe – against a powerful conquest nation. It was a war that had the financial support of England's commercial classes, because the victory of Spain would have snuffed out their dynamic strategy. Conquest and commerce societies cannot coexist.

Unlike the Tudors, the subsequent Stuart dynasty failed to understand that England had been changed forever by the commercial expansion of the sixteenth century and that the monarch was expected by the middle classes to act as the leader of the commerce strategy. By refusing to recall Parliament and by exploiting other sources of funds (customs, feudal revenues, fines, and the sale of honours, the right to collect taxes and crown monopolies), the Stuarts were determined to abandon the strategic leadership of England. Charles I (1625–49) refused not only to defend the commerce strategy in Europe, but even to provide English merchants with protection against their rivals overseas or pirates in local waters. He refused, in his own words, to be 'a Doge of Venice', preferring instead to pursue dynastic wars in Scotland and Europe. It was this blunt refusal to provide strategic leadership that led to the English civil war (1642–48) between King and Parliament.

Even when the Stuart dynasty was restored in 1660 after the death of Oliver Cromwell, they failed to appreciate that they were on trial and that their survival depended on providing effective leadership for the commerce strategy. Charles II (1660–85) not only refused to act as the protector of commerce in Europe, but also maintained close contacts with the conquest strategy of France. After a generation of frustration in the face of kingly intransigence, in 1688 Parliament called upon William of Orange, the effective ruler of the Dutch Republic and defender of the commerce strategy on the Continent, to force James II (1685–88) from the throne.

The change of monarchs in 1688 was called the 'Glorious Revolution', not because of English enthusiasm for the Dutch king but
because at long last the middle classes had found a true leader and
defender of their commerce strategy. To prove it, William III (1689–
1702) and Mary II (1689–94) immediately involved England in the
War of the League of Augsburg against France from 1689 to 1697, and in
the anti-French Wars of Spanish Succession from 1702 to 1713. And
the Commons loved it. They readily agreed to the raising of heavy
land taxes by which the long and expensive wars – much more
expensive than the dynastic wars of the Stuarts – were financed. The
important point is that these wars advanced England's commerce
strategy. When the house of Hanover accepted the English crown in
1714, it did so on Parliament's terms. Never again would a British
monarch misunderstand what was expected of him or her by the
dynamic strategists. The Commons had finally created a monarchy
in their own image.

The third and latest great wave of economic change in Britain, which
began in the mid-eighteenth century, is being driven by the novel
dynamic strategy of technological change. It is this strategy that has
enabled Western Europe to break free from the eternal recurrence. It
is this strategy that has generated the technological paradigm shift
known more widely as the Industrial Revolution. By introducing the
technological strategy, Britain was able to generate extraordinary
profits from new products and new processes within its own borders.
Industrial innovation replaced monopoly access to external resources and markets as the engine of growth. In this way Britain gained
a competitive advantage over its neighbours and created a wealthy
and powerful nation-state that no longer depended heavily on its
overseas possessions. Empire was continued only in order to defend
the technological strategy (through the balance of power concept –
see *The Ephemeral Civilization*), and only until the more economical
nuclear deterrent was developed in the 1940s. After this the British
Empire was quickly dismantled, with no adverse effects on living
standards in the British Isles.

As the technological strategy unfolded, a number of important
institutional changes, driven by strategic demand, took place, including

the transition from a 'limited' to a 'constitutional' monarchy, by which strategic leadership passed from king to Commons, and the emergence of universal suffrage, which placed control of the dynamic strategy in the hands of the entire British people. The struggle to achieve these changes took place in Parliament rather than on the battlefield, as in the mid-seventeenth century. The reasons for this are that all combatants gained from the unfolding technological strategy, and that new and effective leaders emerged in response to the demands of the new strategists.

As the Industrial Revolution took hold the new strategists – the owners of industry, who imitated the commercial gentry by purchasing old estates – increased their representation in Parliament. And as their numbers increased they struggled against the old gentrified commercial interests for control of the dynamic strategy in order to defend and increase their hold over the sources of their wealth. The main battle between these forces in Parliament raged over the Corn Law issue – whether to impose high import duties on wheat – in the 1840s. The reason this did not lead to armed conflict is that the new technological strategy not only provided scope for industrialists to earn extraordinary profits, but also enabled the more entrepreneurial commercial interests to rebuild their fortunes. With the new and cheaper products generated by the technological strategy, British merchants were able to make rapid inroads into overseas markets and, hence, to share in the extraordinary profits of the Industrial Revolution. Only the unenterprising and entrenched commercial gentry, who were able to offer little effective resistance, were finally swept away.

Even the working classes benefited from the technological strategy. While the initial stages of the Industrial Revolution were deskilling, the unfolding technological strategy generated a growing demand for increasing numbers of semiskilled and skilled factory workers. And as these workers began investing time and experience in learning these new skills (human capital) they became increasingly valuable to the industrialists and their real wages began to rise, particularly after 1830. The growing economic and political power of the workers is reflected in the emergence of skilled unions from the 1830s to the 1860s, of semiskilled unions in the 1870s, of 'unskilled' (this is a misnomer – they actually invested in general education and factory skills) unions in the 1880s, and in the extension of the franchise to male householders between 1867 and 1884, to all males in 1918 and to all females in 1928.

In other words, despite the theories of Karl Marx and the rhetoric of the left wing of politics, the workers and the middle classes were not struggling against each other to achieve final victory for different and competing dynamic strategies. Rather they were and are co-strategists because they both have a vested interest in the success of the industrial technological strategy. Both groups have much to lose from its failure. Of course there are differences, but these are confined to the distribution of the surplus generated by a common strategy. In all other respects the political representatives of both groups are called upon to provide the same type of strategic leadership. This is why there has never been and will never be a proletarian revolution in a viable capitalist society. This is why workers fought alongside their capitalist countrymen during the Great War rather than boycott the war in favour of international worker solidarity, as the radical socialists wanted. The workers' interests were national rather than international because they, like the 'capitalists', were concerned to defend their country's dynamic strategy, in which they had a vested interest. There is no such thing as a global dynamic strategy because there are no global strategists. Marx and his followers were wrong because they had an unrealistic dynamic model of human society.

Most observers of England's history over the past millennium have interpreted the succession of 'feudalism', 'mercantile capitalism' and 'industrial capitalism' as a unidirectional and irreversible process. In the same way they regard the emergence of parliamentary democracy as an evolutionary process. Both conclusions are incorrect. The emergence of any one of these societal systems depends on the type of dynamic strategy adopted, which in turn depends on underlying changes in factor endowments, together with the future capacity of the prevailing technological paradigm. The conquest → commerce → technological sequence of Britain was unique and only occurred, as I show in my global history trilogy, because the exhaustion of the commerce strategy coincided with the exhaustion of the global neolithic paradigm. In earlier societies such as ancient Greece and medieval Venice, the strategic sequence was the more typical conquest → commerce → conquest, which led their sociopolitical structures and the process of democratisation to turn back on themselves. And the nature of strategic leadership, as we have seen, closely followed the demands of the strategists.

The United States of America

In the Old World the vehicle of technological change was the nation-state, whereas in the New World the dynamic strategists discovered that they could compete effectively with Western Europe and earn supernormal profits by creating a mega-state. This is the key to understanding the economic, political and social development of the United States. Had it been possible for the founding colonies of North America to generate supernormal profits by employing the nation-state as a strategic vehicle, the mega-state would not have been created. Instead North America would have consisted of a large number of nation-states, in imitation of Western Europe. The civil war of the early 1860s, I argue, was fought on this issue.

The mega-state of North America was formed through the adoption, unfolding and replacement of a number of dynamic strategies originating in the seventeenth century. These strategies include the participation of the American colonies in the British commerce strategy until the 1760s – what I call the dependent-commerce strategy – the family-multiplication strategy, which drove America's westward expansion for a century before 1890, and the technological strategy, which emerged after 1870 and developed exponentially to become the dominant dynamic strategy from the 1890s.

The pursuit of these strategies transformed a handful of small settlements on the east coast of North America at the beginning of the seventeenth century into a mega-state occupying the entire continent between (approximately) the 30th and 45th parallels at the end of the nineteenth century. In this way the United States surpassed Britain in terms of living standards by the end of the First World War, and went on to lead the world in pushing back the global technological frontier in the generation after the Second World War. This was only achieved, however, because of the close relationship between American leaders and the nation's dynamic strategists.

The driving force behind the United States' economic growth and sociopolitical change was the unfolding sequence of dependent-commerce → family multiplication → technological change. The first of these was a spin-off from the English commerce strategy examined above, which was responsible for planting the initial and most successful colonies on the east coast of North America. Once these colonies had been successfully established, in order to serve the commercial interests of the mother country, local entrepreneurs participated in the English strategy as junior players. While they derived benefits from English investment, markets and security, they were constrained by overall objectives formulated in and administered from London. They had no say in English policy making. Indeed English strategic leadership took little notice of the colonial strategists.

America's dependent-commerce strategy came to an end in the last quarter of the eighteenth century when the colonists successfully rebelled against the mother country. The fundamental reason for this rebellion, which was first exposed in *The Ephemeral Civilization* (1997), was Britain's refusal to provide the American strategists with the strategic leadership they demanded. In other words the revolution was an outcome of the clash between two competing dynamic strategies. Although the birth and development of the American colonies in the seventeenth and early eighteenth centuries was the direct outcome of the English/British commerce strategy, an alternative dynamic strategy, this one American-born, began to emerge in the mid-eighteenth century. This new dynamic was the American family-multiplication strategy, which involved the settlement of new land through the process of new family formation, initially through high fertility rates and then, after 1812, massive immigration. It was this dynamic that powered the great westward movement of the American frontier.

But Britain, which pursued a sea-based rather than a land-based dynamic strategy, attempted to block this western expansion through a series of proclamations in 1763, 1768 and 1774, with the intention of restricting settlement to the eastern seaboard. As I show in *The Ephemeral Civilization*, it was this struggle over strategic leadership rather than the irritating taxation imposts of the British that led to the American War of Independence (1775–83). By winning this war, at a cost that greatly exceeded the value of British imposts over the lifetime of the revolutionaries, the Americans gained control of their own dynamic strategy and of the immensely rich rewards that it promised over their, and many future, lifetimes. And these rewards were realised, but only because the new American government provided effective strategic leadership. They did this by financing the exploration of the continent (Lewis and Clark 1803–6); by extending the borders of American society by purchasing Louisiana from Napoleon Bonaparte in 1803, by taking Texas and the south-west from Mexico in 1845 and 1848, by acquiring Oregon Territory in 1846, and by purchasing Arizona from Mexico in 1853; by making this land cheaply available to the rush of new immigrants; and by heavily subsidising transport and communications to integrate this vast land mass into a viable mega-market.

The American Civil War (1861–65) was, as I argue in *The Ephemeral Civilization*, also a struggle for control over America's dynamic strategy, this time by two very different groups of American strategists. By the mid-nineteenth century the North had, for about two generations, pursued an industrialisation programme linked to the expansion of the domestic mega-market. They were more highly urbanised and industrialised, paid higher wages and wanted to impose high tariffs to exclude British manufactured goods. In contrast the South was locked into a dependent-commerce strategy, by which it supplied raw cotton to feed British industrialisation. It consisted of a collection of rural societies based on slave labour, and it rejected protective tariffs because these only increased the cost of importing manufactured goods from Britain and the North.

Owing to these competing strategies, the North and the South possessed fundamentally different attitudes towards the future political structure of North America. The North was committed to the concept of union, but only because its dynamic strategy required the development of a large and highly integrated market. As any fragmentation of that market would threaten their supernormal profits, the strategists of the North were determined to preserve the Union at all costs. In other words the North was irrevocably committed to the idea of the North American mega-market.

The South did not share this commitment. While Southern strategists were keen to participate in the westward expansion, because of the supernormal profits that could be made by exploiting the new land through farming or breeding slaves – the very reason they fought alongside the North in the War of Independence – the longrun progress of the South depended more on its economic relationship with Britain than with the rest of America. The South, therefore, was just as determined to pursue its dependent-commerce strategy, even as a separate country (or countries) if the cost of remaining in the Union rose to unacceptable levels. It favoured the concept of the nation-state, as in Europe, rather than the mega-state relentlessly pursued by the North.

The real source of conflict between the North and the South, therefore, was not the 'moral' issue of slavery as conventional wisdom tells us, but the fundamentally different and conflicting dynamic strategies to which they were totally committed. Slavery was merely the most obvious manifestation of this more fundamental economic difference. While the North rationalised its materialistic pursuit by raising the moral issue of the freedom and dignity of all humans – and there was a small minority that believed this passionately – it would not, and did not, go to war over a moral issue. Similarly the South did not go to war to evangelise its slavery-based system. As the historical record clearly shows, the existence of slavery in the South was not even challenged by the North in the events that led up to the Civil War. That came later as the North attempted to attract others, particularly in Europe, to its cause. The outbreak of war emerged from the determination of the North to prevent the fragmentation of its growing mega-market and was continued – despite the enormous cost in lives (600 000 men) and infrastructure – by both sides to protect and enhance their incompatible dynamic strategies. The Civil War, therefore, was all about the future of strategic leadership in America.

With the victory of the North, the industrialisation of the United States could proceed apace. Rapid industrial development had occurred before 1860, but it was restricted by the size of the domestic market and had largely followed the path laid down by the European Industrial Revolution. Only after the Civil War had been won were the northern industrialists able to fully exploit the American mega-market and, in the process, to make their own contribution to the modern technological strategy. This contribution was the mass production and mass distribution of standardised manufactured commodities. In this they were assisted by governments that understood the importance of strategic leadership. In particular these governments subsidised the building of railroads ahead of demand: in 1860 the United States had only 30 000 miles of railroad, but by 1914 this had increased by a factor of eight to a total of 250 000 miles.

American prosperity increased rapidly between 1870 and 1914, resulting in a doubling of real living standards, and only came to an end in the mid 1920s when the domestic mega-market was finally saturated with locally manufactured products. As we have seen, it was the exhaustion of this technological substrategy that led to the Great Depression, the duration of which was an outcome of the time taken for American strategists to reorient their industrialisation programme towards the world market. This event also demonstrated how governments could panic and lose the plot by listening to economic experts and forgetting their role as strategic leaders. It should have been a warning of things to come.

Once the United States had, in the 1940s, discovered its new substrategy as workshop to the world, it was possible to resume its former rapid growth. It is important to realise that Truman, in contrast to Roosevelt, provided essential strategic leadership in this critical period by introducing the Marshal Plan, which was essentially designed to open global markets for American goods. With this strategic reorientation the United States overcame its former isolationism (a product of its earlier inward-looking substrategy) and took up the global leadership of the technological strategy that had formerly been provided by Britain. It was this leadership role that created the 'golden age' of the 1950s and 1960s and that brought the United States into Cold War confrontation with the USSR as leader of the antistrategic world. But this was only possible because the US government began listening to the strategists again and thereby rediscovered its strategic-leadership role.

Conclusions

From this survey of the past three millennia it is clear that there has always been a close relationship between a society's leader and its strategists. In successful societies, leaders able and willing to serve the interests of their dynamic strategists have always emerged in response to strategic demand. But whenever a political leader has been unable to provide strategic leadership, a crisis has developed and he has been swept away. And there have always been alternative leaders ready and able to fill the void. Had those alternatives not been available, the prevailing dynamic strategy would have collapsed and, in a competitive world, the society in question would have been absorbed by more successful societies. Unless contemporary society can revive its enthusiasm for strategic leadership, this will be our fate too.

5
The Recent Collapse of Strategic Leadership

It is quite clear that the role of strategic leadership has been essential to the success of human civilisations throughout the course of history. Those leaders who failed to understand this fundamental reality led their societies into crisis until, eventually, they were driven out by more perceptive men. In the past there have always been alternative strategic leaders ready to lead their societies out of crisis by facilitating the objectives of their dynamic strategists.

What is so different about the present? The problem for contemporary society is that there are no alternative sources of strategic leadership to call upon in the current real global crisis. While it is possible to change political parties in today's advanced democracies, it is very difficult to change national policies. Our economic experts even argue that strategic leadership – although they do not recognise or understand the concept – is not only unnecessary but also positively dangerous. They preach the omnipotence of individual decision making – an omnipotence that requires no overall direction or support. Governments, they claim, exist only to enforce the rules that these individuals adopt in their business activities. This so-called 'methodological individualism' must be imposed, we are told, on rich and poor countries alike.

It is interesting that strategic leadership is still to be found in some Third World countries that have already set out on the development process – what I call, in *Global Transition* (1999), the **emerging strategic countries** (ESCs). Political leaders in ESCs, like those during the earlier stages of the development of the West, still understand that their best interests will be served by facilitating the objectives of their strategists, who constitute a relatively small ruling elite. Tragically, leaders in the developing world are being forced to relinquish this role during the present 'Asian crisis' by those international agents of neoliberalism the IMF and the World Bank, which are determined to impose totally inappropriate 'structural adjustment' policies and advanced democratic political structures on these struggling societies. As soon as they are able, Asian leaders will reject neoliberal economic and political policies and return to developing their societies along lines similar to those taken by the West at the same stage in the transition process. But until then the West will merely prolong the difficulties that Third World countries are currently experiencing.

A fatal forgetfulness

When did the leaders of Western civilisations forget the essential role of strategic leadership? A study of contemporary history suggests that it was a very recent event. This is reflected in the type of policies pursued by the major rich countries and in their recent economic performance.

Only since the early 1980s – from the early days of the Thatcher and Reagan administrations – have Western governments abandoned their strategic-leadership role. At that time it became fashionable to believe that the best of all worlds could be achieved simply by dismantling the organisations of strategic leadership and selling off the associated infrastructure with indecent haste and at bargain prices to private interests. This is so familiar to us all that it does not require documentation. Only over the past few decades has it been fashionable to assume that the strategists can lead themselves. This is a curious fashion because, as we have seen, it flies in the face of human experience over the past two million years. There is a potentially tragic irony here. The Western world, after being locked in a mortal struggle with the communist world for much of the twentieth century, finally defeated those antistrategic forces only to see them reemerge in more subtle form among their own ranks as neoliberal policies.

What accounts for the fatal forgetfulness? While there are a number of reasons, some of which were touched upon earlier, they are essentially outcomes of the unfolding industrial paradigm. They are, in other words, a product of the modern global dynamic. As our modern technological paradigm has unfolded, and hence as prosperity and liberty have progressed, the complexity of our sociopolitical structures has increased and the quality of our political leadership has declined.

It was argued earlier that the modern fragmentation of society's dynamic strategists into a large number of relatively small competing groups has made the task of identifying its strategic objectives more difficult. The continuous process of democratisation has enabled most of these groups to find representation in parliament. This is particularly so in countries with voting systems based on proportional representation – that is, where the proportion of the vote received by a minority party is translated into the same proportion of seats in parliament.

A good illustration of the impact of proportional representation is the differential success of the minority Green Party in the German (proportional representation) and French (non-proportional representation) systems. In these two countries, at the end of the 1990s the Green Party attracted the same proportion, about 6.8 per cent, of the total votes. In France this provided the Greens with only six seats, whereas in Germany it resulted in as many as 47 seats, enabling the Greens to form a coalition government with the socialists.

This electoral fragmentation has had a number of unfortunate consequences. First, political leaders are distracted from strategic objectives by the political demands of many small groups insisting upon satisfaction of more immediate concerns such as redistribution of resources, preservation of the environment, gender and ethnic rights, and the provision of health, welfare, educational and aged services. Secondly, the electoral pressure to ensure that each small pressure group has direct representation in parliament means that parliamentarians are not necessarily chosen for their strategic leadership qualities.

In addition to electoral fragmentation, the task of government became less clear-cut during the last quarter of the twentieth century because, by then, much of the physical fabric of the technological strategy had been laid down in Western societies. The type of public infrastructure required today is of a more subtle and sophisticated kind than in the past, even the relatively recent past. In the case of conquest societies such as Rome, for example, it was quite obvious that the state needed to invest in an efficient fighting force, communication systems, an effective road network and a reliable navy to move armies quickly around the empire, in an imperial administration, and in the necessary education and training to make all of this operational. In the case of commerce societies such as Venice, Holland and England it was clear that the state needed to provide adequate docking and warehouse facilities, an efficient system of communications, an effective navy and army to defend their strategy, and the establishment of colonies and fortified trading posts throughout the known world. Even in technological societies before the mid-twentieth century it was obvious that the state needed to invest in, or heavily subsidise, a railway network, a telegraph system, urban and industrial infrastructure, and appropriate educational and training facilities. Today, as will be discussed in detail in Chapter 8, governments need to take the lead in providing facilities for the generation of more sophisticated human capital, for more advanced scientific and applied research and, most importantly, for new strategic ideas. As these inputs are less intuitively obvious, contemporary leadership requires a new understanding of the way in which modern economies work.

While lip-service is paid to some of these matters, today's politicians find it more difficult than their forefathers to believe in the benefits that strategic investment provides. It is easier to recognise the potential returns from investment in canals, railways and roads than those from investment in less tangible goods such as higher education, science and the arts. This is reflected in the recent reduction in real public funding, particularly on a per capita basis, devoted to these activities throughout the Western world. Rather than facilitating the technological strategy, contemporary governments are actually running down this strategic infrastructure. And because scientists (both natural and social), intellectuals and their supporters are thinly distributed throughout the electorate they have little political influence and, hence, are unable to prevent this deskilling process. The university/research sector has no political clout and, therefore, can be safely ignored. Responding to narrow interest groups has replaced strategic leadership in contemporary society.

This fatal forgetfulness has led to tragicomic scenes in Western parliaments. While the governments of rich countries no longer know what they should be spending money on, they still preside over highly effective revenue-raising machinery. In some cases this has led to the emergence of large budget surpluses. For some governments, surplus maximisation has become the major political objective. Anything that contributes to the surplus is good, and anything that reduces it is bad. To such governments, the surplus has come to be regarded as some sort of magic pudding. Hence the centrepiece of their economic policy has become the machinery by which taxation is raised. Even opposition parties have been drawn into this curiously primitive game. Battles in the parliaments of these countries are not about the nature of strategic leadership but about the design of the taxation system. Members comically compete with each other for the role of defender of the magic pudding. What they fail to understand, because of the limitations of neoliberal advice, is that a large surplus is a sign not of political success but of strategic failure. And it promotes the self-destruction of participating governments.

These problems have been exacerbated by the declining quality of contemporary political leaders. In Chapter 4 it was noted that strategic leaders of the past were not only tough, ruthless, highly ambitious and energetic, but also highly intelligent, unusually imaginative and, most significant of all, sensitive to the needs of the dynamic strategists. Those who did not have these qualities were eliminated in the strategic struggle. It is hardly surprising, therefore, that strategic leaders were by far the most wealthy and powerful individuals in their societies.

How do the leaders of today rate in this company? They might be ambitious, energetic and ruthless – although probably not to the same degree as their counterparts in the past – but they appear to lack the appropriate imagination and essential sensitivity to the requirements of the dynamic strategists. Certainly they are not the most wealthy and personally powerful individuals in their society and they cannot nominate their successors (particularly their offspring). Those more able individuals are to be found in the corporate sector. Even the President of the United States can be impeached for having a sexual affair and attempting to cover it up. What would the emperors of Rome have thought of this or, more scandalously, of the President's extremely modest salary? More pertinently, what would any corporate baron in the United States today think privately of this? Or even the leaders of Third World nations, who are certainly the most wealthy and powerful individuals in their own societies? And great wealth and power can only be passed down through the family if you are a corporate baron like Rupert Murdoch, not if you are an elected president like Bill Clinton. Wealth, power and leadership qualities in advanced societies today are to be found outside the political system.

False prophets

The uncertainty, even confusion, of today's politicians has led them to seek assistance from economic experts – the false prophets of the contemporary world. In doing so our political leaders have adopted the neoliberal vision not only of the modern economy but also of the role of the state. The so-called 'new political economy' of the late twentieth century – associated with economists such as James Buchanan (Nobel laureate), Gordon Tulloch and Marcus Olsen – has charted a new role for modern government.

These 'new' political economists believe, in the tradition of Adam Smith, that the role of government should be restricted to protecting individuals and property rights, and to enforcing private contracts. No more and no less. Any government exceeding this role will, they argue, create wasteful social activity in the form of public and private 'rent-seeking' (the seeking of unproductive surpluses). In this way governments will grow out of control by attempting to maximise revenue, unconstrained as they are by 'moral rules', and private lobby groups will invest time and resources in their attempt to persuade leading politicians to redistribute income in favour of the lobbyists through tariffs, subsidies, tax concessions and export bounties. The end result, they tell us, is to divert resources from their most efficient use. Only small and non-interventionist governments can prevent this. In the absence of 'moral rules' this minimal state role can be achieved only through the imposition of 'constitutional rules' devised by intellectuals!

The historical evidence marshalled in Chapter 4 clearly shows that the emasculated state proposed by the 'new political economics' would be incapable of providing the strategic leadership that successful states have always shown by spearheading the prevailing dynamic strategy. Such a state could not possibly play any dynamic role in the real world. In this completely unrealistic, libertarian vision there is no role for dynamic strategies, strategic demand or strategic leadership. It is a vision of the world that requires a passive, not a dynamic, role for governments. Like the neoclassical mainstream, their emphasis is on static efficiency rather than dynamic progress.

The neoliberal vision is unrealistic because it is the outcome of deductive guesswork – of intellectual gameplaying. It is contradicted by the evidence of reality. Our systematic study of the role of the state throughout history shows, by contrast, that in the real dynamic world the state plays an indispensable role in facilitating the objectives of the dynamic strategists. It is an inescapable fact that, in a successful society, strategic leadership is provided by the representatives of the strategists for the benefit of the strategists.

What will be the consequences?

The future consequences of this recent collapse in strategic leadership will be grave. A society that has abandoned strategic leadership is a society headed for stagnation and, unless the problem is rectified, collapse. We will witness not an orderly, efficient society in a state of equilibrium, but an increasingly moribund society descending into a state of chaos. It is like an imagined attempt to prevent the earth spinning on its axis: if it could be achieved the attempt would lead to a collapse of life on our planet. Those who want to eliminate strategic leadership harbour an unconscious but very real death wish.

Our modern civilisation is unique. We are threatening to do what no other civilisation in the past 11 000 years has been foolish enough to even contemplate – to abandon strategic leadership. Ours will be the first civilisation in either the Old or New World to collapse *before* exhausting its dominant dynamic strategy. Quite an achievement! In the past, great civilisations only stagnated, declined and collapsed when the material potential of their dynamic strategies had been used up and they were unable to replace them with new strategies. No civilisation in the past was ever stricken with the contemporary disease of the fatal forgetfulness.

What lies beyond the wilful destruction of the technological strategy? What lies beyond is the reemergence of war and conquest. As I show in my global history trilogy, the collapse of either the commerce or the technological strategy can, in the face of the universal desire to survive and prosper, lead only to the pursuit of the conquest strategy.

The consequences for our generation of such an outcome are disturbing to contemplate. It will involve great loss of life – probably on a scale that would make even Roman emperors catch their breath – great and irreparable destruction of the natural environment and, to confound the social evolutionists, a reversal of the process of democratisation in the political, social and economic spheres.

From this chaos will emerge a great irony. If it survives, human society will inevitably rediscover the role of strategic leadership. It will be a kind of strategic leadership known not to modern man but only to men of the past such as Alexander the Great, Julius Caesar, Augustus, Attila the Hun, William the Conqueror, Genghis Khan, Moteuczomah the Aztec, Cortes the Spaniard and Napoleon Bonaparte. It will be the strategic leadership of the conqueror. This rediscovery, however, will come too late to save Western civilisation.

Can collapse be avoided?

The short answer to the above question is yes, but only if we change our vision of the purpose of the state and rediscover the role of strategic leadership. And soon. As the fatal forgetfulness is a natural outcome of the process of democratisation driven by the unfolding industrial technological paradigm, and as no right-thinking person would want to reverse that process, we need to develop and promote an awareness of the true nature of the dynamics of human society. This involves abandoning the neoliberal deductive approach and adopting the stratological inductive approach to policy formulation. This approach will be considered in detail in the remainder of the book.

6
An End to Progress and Liberty?

The triumph of the crisis makers poses a threat not only to material progress but also to personal liberty. These two staples of modern society are inextricably bound together. As the dominant dynamic strategy unfolds they advance together, and as it stagnates they retreat together. The growing pluralisation of modern society, as we have seen, leads us to forget the importance of longrun dynamics and the essential role of strategic leadership. And through our forgetfulness we unintentionally prepare the way for an end to progress and liberty. For who can remind us when our so-called experts – the orthodox economists – have failed to understand these things?

While the strategists understand intuitively that governments are failing them, they are unable to change the system. They can change governments but not government policy. It is a problem, I have argued, that has become critical in the past decade because orthodox economic knowledge has assumed a monolithic character. Today there is only one economic view of the world and only one policy. The problem is that both are entirely misleading. This has created a very dangerous condition in modern democracy that I call the **frustration of the strategists**. For in their frustration the strategists of some vanguard countries are turning increasingly to the political underworld to resolve the current impasse. This is a condition that will soon emerge in countries throughout the Western world *if governments continue to pursue deforming neoliberal policies.*

The frustration of the strategists

Strategists are the driving force in human society. In our modern world, therefore, they are the creators of progress and liberty. But when frustrated by wilfully obstructive governments they are responsible for creating political systems that may promise release but in fact lead only to the curtailment of liberty and, ultimately, progress. In other words the frustration of the strategists generates a political cycle that can and will eliminate the progress and liberty that are characteristic of the technological strategy in its mature phase. The frustration of the strategists, which expresses itself in an increasing incidence of strikes and political volatility, is an outcome of the fatal forgetfulness.

In theory the ballot box determines government policy. The usual argument is that the party in opposition will learn from the mistakes of an unpopular government and will, on gaining office, change official policy. But in our contemporary world the logic of reasonable people is confounded. All major parties have been persuaded that there is only one valid view of the economic world and only one set of policies, and that these are those outlined by the neoliberal experts. Hence instead of competing with each other to facilitate the technological strategy, each mainstream party competes to be more neoliberal than the rest. This can be seen in election after election throughout the Western world since the early 1980s.

At each election we delude ourselves that the incoming politicians will have learnt from the mistakes of their outgoing colleagues. Our delusions, however, are invariably shattered. Despite their expressions of heartfelt concern about unemployment, new governments soon succumb to pressure from the crisis makers and end up pursuing neoliberal policies with more rigour than their opponents. They come to believe that the failure of their political opponents was due not to the type of policies they pursued but to the determination with which they pursued them. In the end it matters not that the parties in any political system are of the right or the left, because in the end the neoliberal experts have their way.

To what quarter should the strategists turn? None of the major parties, even those offering some Keynesian policies (mixed up with neoliberal philosophy), seem to understand the frustration of the strategists. The only support comes from the political underworld –

from the radical right. These radical groups, which are driven by economically irrational objectives, arise from the underworld because they sense that there are opportunities to be exploited in the growing dissatisfaction of mainstream electorates. They are willing to oppose orthodox policies and to propose radical solutions to the problems of the strategists in order to reap the support of the disaffected. The fact that they express their objectives and prejudices in the crudest fashion actually helps to maximise their support as it plays on natural prejudices. Their ideas are both unorthodox, which is their strength, and hopelessly uninformed, which is their weakness. Only as the radical right gathers strength as a political force does it attract opportunistic 'experts', who are able to fashion these ad hoc ideas into a more consistent and sophisticated doctrine.

While the policies of the radical right appear to offer a way out for the frustrated strategists, they are ultimately destructive of their cause and, hence, of society. It is instructive to compare the radical right with the crisis makers who have given them their place in the sun. Unlike the policies of the radical right, those of the crisis makers are rational in an economic sense. Their proponents are concerned that society should maximise its material returns as effectively as possible. The problem is that these policies are based on a total misunderstanding of reality. In contrast the radical right usually adopts irrational objectives, such as a racial agenda – 'purifying' the racial stock by repatriating ethnic groups. The classic case, which is discussed in detail below, was the National Socialist (Nazi) Party in Germany during the interwar period. The Nazi Party was concerned to maximise not the materialist objectives of German strategists but the racial aims of its leader, Adolf Hitler. A society that delivers itself into the hands of the radical right will self-destruct because its pursuit of irrational objectives either brings it into conflict with other societies or leads it to exercise an unsustainable tyranny over its strategists.

I argue that there is evidence in the contemporary world of the reemergence of antistrategic forces of the type that overwhelmed Germany in the 1930s. This will surprise some readers, who may argue that world conditions today are not comparable to those of the interwar period. Certainly the world at the turn of the century is, in a superficial way, very different from that of the 1920s and where there are some similarities, such as high levels of unemployment and unstable international financial markets, the situation now is not as severe as then. But appearances deceive.

All that is required to set in train the emergence of the darker forces of politics is the complete frustration of the strategists. This can be achieved just as effectively with an apparently low-key orthodox policy as with a few international king hits. Economic vitality can be destroyed with a thousand small cuts as well as by one stroke of the executioner's axe. The severity of the problem is to be measured in terms of the degree of strategist frustration rather than the rate of unemployment. At the moment the degree of strategic frustration differs between countries. It is probably at its highest in Austria, France, Switzerland and Australia. If the Western world continues to follow the neoliberal vision, the frustration of the strategists will inevitably emerge in other countries as well. And soon.

The classic case of strategic frustration – Nazi Germany

Germany in the interwar period is the classic case of an advanced technological society losing its way through the abandonment of strategic leadership, frustration of the strategists and submission to the political forces of darkness. While it is an extreme case, it nevertheless illustrates the *process* that is beginning to take place in contemporary society as neoliberal governments increasingly frustrate the strategists of the Western world.

The frustration of German strategists during the interwar years was an outcome of the Treaty of Versailles of 1919, which determined the conditions under which the First World War was to be concluded. This settlement prevented the Weimar Republic's Social Democratic government from providing the strategic leadership that was required to revive Germany's dynamic strategy. The Great Depression merely provided the finishing stroke that finally destroyed the attempts of the Social Democrats to reconstruct Germany's economy, delivering the strategists into the hands of the Nazi Party. This brought an immediate end to liberty and, within a few years, to progress. The strategists had been hoodwinked.

The Treaty of Versailles made it impossible for the German strategists to resume their earlier technological pursuit. In the first place the attitude of the Allies, particularly the French, weakened the Weimar government to the point where it was unable to facilitate the objectives of the German middle class or to resist the pressure of the small but powerful former ruling elite, consisting of big businessmen, large landowners and army officers. Secondly, the immense reparations imposed on Germany – amounting to 152 billion marks or $US33 billion – effectively crippled the German economy. The federal government found it impossible to finance its expenditure from normal sources of revenue. During the second half of 1923, for example, the government's revenue on a monthly basis ranged from just 0.09 per cent to 18.2 per cent of its expenditure. In order to cover this huge budgetary deficit, the federal government resorted to printing paper money. And the state and local governments, together with many industrial and commercial enterprises, did the same. During 1923 the notes in circulation, which included up to two thousand different currencies, increased from 1.3 thousand billion marks in January to 400 267 640 thousand billion marks in December. It is this that fuelled the hyperinflation of that year, destroying the savings of the middle and working classes. Hyperinflation, in other words, is the outcome not of rapid economic growth, as the neoliberals tell us, but of strategic collapse.

The problem of reparations was compounded by the non-compliance and outright hostility of the old ruling elite, who not only withdrew their political support but also refused to accept the imposition of direct taxes, actively evaded the payment of other taxes, and engineered the capital flight that precipitated Germany's exchange rate crisis. The rent-seekers had, they thought, much to gain from the hyperinflation that they had helped to generate, because it eliminated both their old debts and the emerging new strategists. The Weimar government was so preoccupied with its own survival that it was unable to defend Germany's strategists.

The hyperinflation of 1923 was finally brought under control by the Dawes Plan, which stabilised the mark by arranging an international loan to meet government debts, set more realistic reparation targets and negotiated a French/Belgian withdrawal from the Ruhr. But the relative prosperity of Germany between 1924 and 1929 was a false dawn. It was based largely on a flourishing of monopoly capitalism – rent-seeking by big business – made possible by the power grabbing of large industrial concerns during the early 1920s when the Weimar government was distracted by issues of survival. While there was some spillover for the population at large in the form of housing improvements and social benefits, this merely cloaked the fact that Germany's dynamic strategy had stalled and that real economic and political power was held by the old rent-seekers rather than the new profit-seekers – by the antistrategists rather than the strategists. This was reflected in the election of the arch-conservative Hindenburg to the presidency in 1925.

Only a government able to throw off these crippling external controls and to exercise effective leadership would be able to get Germany moving again. Had the international economy entered into a 'golden age', like that experienced after the Second World War, and had the Allies scrapped reparations and allowed Germany to control its own destiny, it is likely that Germany's dynamic strategy would have revived during the 1930s. But as we know that was not to be. The Allies remained bloody-minded to the end, refusing to abandon reparations until July 1932, when there was no other option and when it was far too late. At the German federal elections in that month, almost 40 per cent of the population made their pact with the forces of darkness. The final straw was the impact of the American depression after late 1929.

The disruption caused by the Great Depression was particularly severe in Germany owing to its extremely debilitated condition. Unemployment increased from three million in February 1929 to upwards of nine million in January 1933. This amounted to a staggering rate of unemployment of 43.8 per cent compared with 24.9 per cent in the United States, 22.1 per cent in the United Kingdom, 26.6 per cent in Canada and 28.1 per cent in Australia. The middle and working classes, who had lost their savings in the hyperinflation of 1923 and had struggled to rebuild them in the second half of that decade, were finally made destitute by this massive increase in unemployment and the corresponding reduction in consumer demand.

But the most conspicuous casualty was the Social Democratic government, which was pushed to the wall in March 1930 by the representatives of the army, heavy industry and big property. According to Geoffrey Barraclough in *The Origins of Modern Germany* (p. 450), one leading industrialist is reported to have said of the Great Depression: '*This is the crisis we need*'. (We will have reason to return to this expression when examining the situation today.) Thereafter government, exercised by decree, was taken over by the temporarily triumphant old ruling elite under Hindenburg and the army. To finance their activities they increased indirect taxes and import duties and imposed a new poll tax. Those familiar with neoliberal policies will not be surprised that their development policy consisted of expanding exports through severe economic deflation.

The burden of this authoritarian government fell squarely on the defeated strategists rather than on the victorious rent-seekers. Indeed large subsidies were paid out to bankrupt *Junker* farmers east of the Elbe. This was naked antistrategic policy carried out in the interests of the old ruling elite. It finally destroyed any hope that the German strategists may have entertained.

This final frustration of the German strategists had a spectacular political outcome. In the election of 1924 Adolf Hitler's National Socialist Party received only 0.9 million votes, but in September 1930 it won 6.5 million, and in July 1932 as many as 13.7 million, or 37.4 per cent of the electorate. No one expected this rapid expansion in the support of the radical right, but it is the type of outcome predicted by my dynamic-strategy model.

The remarkable change in the political fortunes of the Nazi Party in less than a decade was largely because of the defection of the middle classes from their traditional parties. The number of votes for middle-class parties (excluding the Catholic Centre Party) declined over the same decade from 13.2 to 4.0 million. Interestingly, working-class voters were attracted not to the radical right (the Nazi Party) but to the radical left (the Communist Party). Quite clearly the rise in the fortunes of the Nazi Party was an outcome of the frustration of Germany's middle-class strategists.

Hitler, despite falling somewhat short of an electoral majority, was able to attain power 'legally' by the greedy and inept machinations of the old ruling elite. As they found themselves in mid 1932 without any electoral support, Hindenburg and his Chancellor, Franz von Papen, attempted to gain some legitimacy for their dictatorship by inviting Hitler to become Chancellor from 30 January 1933. With this act the rational technological strategy was formally abandoned and replaced with the irrational conquest strategy. Conquest is irrational in the modern era for rich societies because the returns to investment in the technological strategy are both higher in the long-run and much less risky. Hitler pursued conquest not to facilitate the material objectives of the strategists but to implement his own irrational desire for the renewal and expansion of the German 'race'.

In 1933 German liberty was at an end, and progress was soon to follow. For a brief season, however, prosperity returned. Hitler's preparations for war rapidly reduced the number of men unemployed, and his welfare programme aimed at renewing the German race improved the well-being of the average person. His conquest strategy also improved the living standards of the German people between 1939 and 1943 through pillage, requisitioning, forced labour and a massive land-grab. Something like 25 million tons of food were requisitioned from occupied Europe, thereby increasing the German civilian ration by 20–25 per cent. Only after 1943, following the failure of the campaign against the USSR, did the German people begin to suffer material hardship. Only then did the middle classes begin to regret throwing their support behind Hitler and his promises to eliminate the frustration of the strategists.

It was not until after the Second World War, when the Allies refused to repeat the mistakes of the fathers of the Treaty of Versailles and the world economy entered into a 'golden age' of prosperity, that the western part of Germany was able to refire a technological strategy that had slowly but steadily been extinguished between 1914 and 1933. This was only possible because Germany's new democratic government was able, with considerable material assistance from the West, to rediscover its role as strategic leader.

Signs of the underworld in the present – the radical right

What does it take to cause the strategists to switch their support from mainstream parties to the political underworld of the radical right? Not as much as many observers believe. Most commentators focus on the drama of external events and ignore the real underlying causes. This is because they do not possess a realistic dynamic model of human society. Such a model tells us that the only matter essential to the success of the political underworld – the threat to liberty – is the frustration of the strategists. This need not be the outcome of cataclysmic events as it was for Germany during the interwar period. World war and global depression are not necessary conditions. Indeed the causes of the frustration of the strategists can be much more subtle.

It is this subtle suppression of the strategists that we can see in the Western world today. A subtle suppression arising from the imposition of neoliberal policies that are sapping the energy of those responsible for our progress. It is death by a thousand cuts rather than one dramatic blow. How many more times will the strategists rise after being slashed with such great finesse by the crisis makers?

The canary in the coalmine – the Australian case

There are worrying signs that the political underworld is beginning to reemerge in the West. It is well known that a number of European countries – such as France, Belgium, Austria and Germany – have well-established radical-right (usually called far-right) parties. While they have been part of the political scenery for the past generation, with the exception of Austria (22 per cent) they have failed to break out of the so-called '15 per cent ghetto' of national votes. The reason is that, until recently, the conservative parties in these countries have been able to rule in their own right. Now that more radical groups on the left, often in coalition, have gained power in major countries such as France and Germany, we can expect that centre-right parties, in an effort to oust left-wing governments, will flirt with the radical right (as they did in Germany in the early 1930s). There is some evidence that this has been happening recently in France. At the same time, the radical right will increase their share of the national vote as left-wing governments continue to frustrate the ambitions of the strategists. But this is in the future. A current indicator of the frustration of the strategists by neoliberal policies is the case of Australia – a country with a long history of democratic government, free from extremism in politics on either the right or the left.

Australia, I argue, is the Western world's early warning system. It is the canary in the political coalmine. In just two years the radical right has emerged as an established and influential political force for the first time in Australia's history. Australia's middle-of-the-road approach to politics was, for example, not even disturbed during the Great Depression, when up to one-third of the workforce was unemployed. This international crisis was regarded by the strategists as something beyond the control of their political leaders. When governments changed during the Depression, the incoming group did its best to support the strategists on the land and in the cities. It was a time in that country when the politicians listened to what their electorates wanted, and they competed to be the first to provide it.

This attitude was enshrined in its party structure: the rural interests were effectively represented by the Country (now called the National) Party, the urban middle classes by the (conservative) Liberal Party and the working classes by the Australian Labor Party (ALP). At this time there was no need to systematically consult the views of the economic experts who, in any case, were very few in number.

Only since the 1980s have these parties lost sight of their strategic purpose and substituted the neoliberal ideas of the economic experts for the needs of the Australian strategists. The first to change in this respect, somewhat surprisingly, was the ALP. After the election of the Hawke Labor government in 1983, the new administration began with a traditional labour/Keynesian policy emphasis, but within a year had adopted the neoliberal policy approach advocated by mainstream economic experts. Ironically these were the policies pioneered by the Conservative Thatcher government in the UK and the Republican Reagan administration in the United States. Interestingly the neoliberal policies of the ALP were studied carefully by Tony Blair, the Labour leader in the UK, before he came to power in May 1997.

This about-turn in political vision and policy was bewildering not only to the ALP's traditional working-class supporters but also to the conservative opposition. In a very real sense the ALP moved to the right of the Liberal (if not the National) Party, which at the time was dominated by 'small l' liberals (called 'wets'), led by Malcolm Fraser and Andrew Peacock. The effect of this dramatic transformation of the political arena was to cause an ideological split in the Liberal Party as the neoliberals (called 'drys'), led by John Howard, emerged to meet the ALP challenge. In the process of this ideological battle, which helped to keep the conservatives out of power for thirteen years, both the Liberal and the National Party lost sight of their strategic purpose. The change in the name of the farmers' party from 'Country' to 'National' symbolises this.

The Hawke/Keating ALP governments (1983–96), in their pursuit of the neoliberal vision, also lost contact with Australian strategists. They had won office (after eight years of conservative rule) in the middle of a recession, when unemployment was 10.5 per cent and real GDP was growing negatively (–2 per cent per annum). This was the legacy of the Fraser government, in which John Howard was Treasurer. By mid 1989 the unemployment rate had been reduced to 6 per cent and real GDP was growing at over 5 per cent owing to an initial phase of expansionary fiscal policy and lower rates of interest. While this was fairly Keynesian in inspiration, the government also attempted, in neoclassical vein, to reduce real wages. The transition was not yet complete.

But from this time the Hawke/Keating regime came increasingly under the influence of neoliberal advisers. About the middle of 1988 monetary policy was tightened in an effort to reduce both the deficit on current account and the rate of inflation, which was running at 6–7 per cent (down from 11 per cent when the ALP had won office). While in strategic terms neither issue was a real problem, the nominal rate of interest was increased in a large number of steps until it peaked at 18.4 per cent in September/October 1989. As a direct result of this deflationary neoliberal policy, unemployment rose steadily from 6 per cent in June 1989 to 11.4 per cent in February 1993, real GDP growth fell from 5 per cent in mid 1989 to –2 per cent in early 1991, and the inflation rate fell from 6 per cent in mid 1989 to 1.5 per cent in mid 1991.

Despite the deterioration of all economic indicators during 1989 and 1990, despite the difficulties being deliberately imposed on Australian strategists and despite the derailment of Australia's dynamic strategy, Paul Keating, Australia's Treasurer (by his own admission, 'the best treasurer in the world') cheerfully and enthusiastically defended his policies and continued to pursue a deflationary course. His biographer, John Edwards, tells us of the satisfaction that Keating derived from seeing 'capitalists' going bankrupt as interest rates rose. When the wisdom of his policy was challenged, Keating responded with his famous, neoliberal-inspired statement: '*This is the recession we had to have*.' The similarity between this remarkable statement and that made by a leading member of the old German ruling elite at the beginning of the Great Depression, as they deliberately destroyed the democratic Weimar Republic, will not be lost on the careful reader. It is the typical response of those who have lost sight of the real role of government, which is strategic leadership.

The Australian federal election of 1993 was an excellent opportunity to remove the antistrategic Keating government. (Paul Keating, the minister most closely associated with the ALP's neoliberal policies, had taken over the prime ministership from Bob Hawke in 1991.) Had the conservative opposition been more in touch with their own strategic supporters they would have won the election in a landslide.

Unfortunately for Australia, the Liberal Party had been hijacked by the neoliberals. At the time of this election the new Liberal leader was John Hewson, a former professor of neoclassical economics at the University of New South Wales and a former adviser to John Howard.

Instead of fighting the 1993 election on behalf of Australia's beleaguered strategists, Hewson, with typical neoliberal myopia, decided it was time to introduce a regressive goods and services (or value-added) tax. Whenever there is a problem in the economy, the neoliberals believe that a good dose of austerity is the only remedy. If there is no pain there can be no gain. The value-added tax proposal was a gift to Keating, who managed to wrong-foot Hewson repeatedly over its details and to divert the electorate's attention from the real issue of strategic leadership. Keating also promised the electorate substantial income tax cuts. Despite expectations to the contrary by most political observers, even the Prime Minister and his staff, the ALP was returned to office with the smallest of margins. What other choice did the strategists have?

But the strategists were not rewarded for their confused loyalty. Faced with a growing deficit (arising from revenue rather than expenditure problems), the Keating government abandoned the promised policies that had narrowly returned it to office: the promised income tax cuts were taken off the agenda and, ironically, regressive consumption taxes were increased in an ad hoc manner. Although Keating formally relinquished responsibility for economic issues and attempted to pose as a statesman on the world (largely East Asian) stage, he was drawn back into economic decision making by his colleagues John Dawkins (Treasurer) and Ralph Willis (Finance Minister). During his final term, Keating, who had had his fingers burnt over his earlier deflationary stance, pursued a less austere monetary policy. Hence nominal interest rates fell, the growth rate of real GDP increased and the rate of inflation rose slightly, but total unemployment refused to fall below 8 per cent or youth unemployment below 40 per cent.

In case it is thought that Keating was a political maverick pursuing his own policy objectives, it is worthwhile considering a retrospective TV programme on the Hawke/Keating regime. When asked by the interviewer why he had pursued a deflationary policy in the late 1980s and early 1990s, Keating replied with unusual candour (because he usually liked to claim that, as 'the world's best treasurer', he had been completely in charge of economic policy) that he had had little choice because he had received the same advice from the Treasury, the Department of Finance, the Reserve Bank and his personal advisers. This effectively illustrates not only the monolithic nature of ortho-dox economics but also what happens to those who follow it blindly.

The long-suffering strategists were to have their revenge. At the Australian federal election of March 1996 the conservative coalition led by John Howard (who had taken over from the accident-prone Alexander Downer, who in turn had replaced the uncomprehending John Hewson) won by a landslide. The Liberal–National coalition won 94 of the 148 House of Representative seats, giving it a margin of 40 seats. Keating's supporters were stunned by the magnitude of the defeat, and even his well-informed and thoughtful biographer, John Edwards, seemed to be at a loss to explain it. Edwards argued that the electorate had grown tired of a political party that had been in power for thirteen consecutive years. But it seems to me that Edwards' loyalty to neoclassical economics (he was a senior econom-ics adviser to the Prime Minister) prevented him from observing and understanding the frustration of the strategists.

But once again, having changed governments the strategists were unable to change policies. The new Liberal–National government took up the neoliberal cause with a vengeance. Its primary objective was to reduce the large deficit inherited from the ALP (similar in size to that passed on to the ALP some 13 years before), even if it meant the destruction of publicly funded institutions in the fields of higher education, science, research and culture. The tragedy is that these institutions are essential to facilitating the unfolding of the techno-logical strategy. Yet none of this matters to a government that has neither the ability nor the intention to provide strategic leadership. The Howard government values sporting institutions (particularly the game of cricket) much more highly than strategic institutions: the greatest living Australian, we are told repeatedly by John Howard, is a cricketer in his nineties! How could it be that the conservative parties, which were in opposition for so long, failed to understand the plight of the strategists and the reason for the ALP's failure? Like the ALP they are captives of neoliberalism.

The key to Liberal–National policy is what happens to inflation. When the rate of inflation begins to increase and appears to be

approaching the predetermined target of 2.5 per cent, monetary policy is employed to deflate the economy. This is standard neoliberal
policy currently enforced throughout the Western world. Economic
growth – which the conservatives do not regard as inconsistent with
their deflationary policies or the downgrading of R&D, technology,
science and higher education – will, they argue, be generated by
supply-side policies such as government withdrawal from economic
enterprise, deregulation, reduction of the power of unions, and
introduction of 'enterprise bargaining'. Owing to this myopic policy,
the rate of unemployment failed to fall below 8 per cent during their
first term in office (1996–8), the rate of growth of GDP declined and
the rate of inflation dropped below zero for a number of quarters in
1998 (always an indicator of strategic derailment). The slight improvement in these indicators at the beginning of the Liberal–National
government's second term of office (1998), is a direct result of the
international market devaluation of the Australian dollar and a consumption boom that is driving down the saving rate, rather than to a
strategic revival. As such it will be fleeting.

What are the strategists to do? Where can they turn when none of
the major parties is willing to take up their cause and provide strategic
leadership? In desperation many turned to a highly unlikely figure –
at least in terms of the Australian political experience – to a former
Liberal Party candidate, Pauline Hanson, who was unhappy with the
immigration and Aboriginal policies of the party hierarchy. Her out-
spokenness on these and other knee-jerk issues led to a breach with
her party but at the same time it struck a chord with many frustrated
strategists, particularly those in rural areas. The public reaction
was so spontaneous and widespread that Hanson formed the One
Nation Party in April 1997. Despite the highly authoritarian nature
of One Nation, it attracted many active supporters and achieved
remarkably rapid electoral success. In the Queensland state election
in June 1998, One Nation won a staggering 22.7 per cent of the
votes, which translated into 11 seats out of the total of 89 (or 12.4
per cent).

The Australian federal election to be held in October 1998 would
be a test of the popularity of Howard's antistrategic policies and of
the future of the radical right. Owing to the magnitude of Howard's
victory just thirty months earlier, no one expected the badly discredited ALP to have any chance of winning. Many, however, doubted

the government's wisdom in fighting the election on the value-added tax issue, just as Hewson, the sorcerer's apprentice, had done unsuccessfully merely five years earlier. But Howard had no choice. He badly needed to divert the electorate's attention away from his failure to provide any form of strategic leadership. His ability to do so, however, depended on whether the ALP, under Kim Beazley's leadership, would treat the value-added tax as the main election issue. Fortunately for Howard they did. Had Beazley campaigned on strategic leadership, I have no doubt he would have won.

As it was, the ALP won 51 per cent of the total votes (on a two-party preferred basis) for the House of Representatives but owing to the distribution of that majority support it failed to win government. With only 49 per cent of the total votes (on a two-party preferred basis) and a reduction of its majority from 40 to 12 seats, the Howard government should recognise that its neoliberal policies have been rejected by the Australian people. Perversely, but predictably, the Prime Minister claims he has a mandate for his antistrategic stance. The rot will continue.

The remarkable new development in Australian federal electoral history – a development that underlines the people's rejection of neoliberal policies – was that the radical right received almost one million votes, amounting to 8.4 per cent of the total cast for the House of Representatives. The distribution of this vote was highest in rural areas and in those states more dependent on rural/mining activities. One Nation won 14.4 per cent of the primary vote in Queensland, 9.8 per cent in New South Wales (with the northern regions indistinguishable from Queensland), but only 3.7 per cent in Victoria and 2.5 per cent in Tasmania.

The 1998 federal election made One Nation the third most popular party after the ALP (40.1 per cent) and the Liberals (33.9 per cent), completely eclipsing the co-ruling National Party (5.3 per cent). Yet despite this ballot box success One Nation failed to gain any seats in the House of Representatives (Pauline Hanson even lost her own), while the National Party won 16. The reason is that the National Party's support is geographically concentrated in the rural areas, whereas One Nation's support is divided between rural and urban areas. Had Australia possessed a proportional voting system in 1998, the National Party would have won only eight seats while One Nation would have won 12. Also, this relatively large vote failed to

translate into senate seats with One Nation winning only one compared with the Democrats' nine.

Many election commentators seem to believe that One Nation has
shot its bolt because it gained only one Senate seat in the 1998
federal election. They claim that it is typical of protest parties that
briefly flash across the political sky. This is confirmed, they say, by
the rebellion in early 1999 of some of the One Nation MPs in
Queensland against the undemocratic nature of the party. In addition, political surveys in early 1999 suggested that public support for
One Nation was falling due to a slight improvement in economic
conditions (owing to the currency devaluation generated, ironically,
by the Asian 'crisis').

Of course One Nation may well self-destruct as an organisation,
owing to incompetent leadership, or it may suffer reverses in the
forthcoming state elections owing to a fortuitous and temporary
improvement in economic conditions. This would not mean that
the problem had gone away. Those that believe this are able to do so
because they have no realistic dynamic model. My dynamic-strategy
model suggests that *unless neoliberal policies are completely abandoned*
the frustration of the strategists will continue and the radical right
will reemerge in the form either of One Nation or some other
extremist right-wing party. It is the frustration of the strategists, generated by the refusal of the mainstream parties to provide strategic
leadership, which is the key to Australia's political future. This is a
matter of worldwide significance, not because Australia is important
at the global level, but because it is providing the early-warning signs
of what will happen throughout the West if, through the enforcement of neoliberal policies, the frustration of the strategist rises to
dangerous levels. We must not be distracted by temporary reversals.

Since writing this, the New South Wales state election has been held
(27 March 1999). Despite early polls predicting a One Nation vote of
only 3.5 per cent, despite the lack of media interest in One Nation
candidates, despite being written off by the so-called 'experts', despite
government pork-barrelling in rural areas, and despite the marginal
(but temporary) reduction in unemployment owing to the devaluation of the Australian dollar, One Nation managed to gain the sup-

port of 7.7 per cent of the total electorate and over 20 per cent in many rural electorates. At the same time the number of independents in the NSW parliament doubled, further reflecting the disillusionment of the strategists with the neoliberal policies of the major parties. It is highly likely that, had the Australian economy not experienced a nonstrategic or 'accidental' growth surge in 1998–99, these independent seats would have been picked up by One Nation, as they will in the future if the growth rate slows and unemployment rises as expected.

The remainder of the First World

It is too early to tell whether the rest of the First World will turn to the radical right as rapidly as the Australians have done. It all depends on whether their governments are able to reject the anti-strategic policies of the neoliberals in favour of strategic leadership. Certainly there are growing signs throughout the First World of the frustration of the strategists. While the radical right is an established presence on the political scene in many of these countries, the strategists appear to be persisting with the mainstream political parties at the present time, but if their frustration continues the radical right will emerge quickly, and liberty will be on the defensive.

Western Europe has witnessed an emphatic reaction on the part of its strategists against the austere neoliberal policies pursued by conservative governments in the 1980s and 1990s. In the past few years conservative governments in Britain (May 1997), France (June 1997) and Germany (October 1998) have been replaced by their left-wing opponents. Today the moderate left controls or co-controls thirteen of the EU's fifteen member countries. Only Ireland and Spain are still ruled by conservative governments. This is the first stage of an attempt by the strategists to force the abandonment of neoliberal policies. The next stage will depend on whether these left-wing governments are able to provide the leadership that the strategists are seeking.

In late 1998 some of the new EU governments were beginning to address the concerns of their electorates about the high level of unemployment (10.8 per cent for the EU, 11.5 per cent in France,

10.8 per cent in Germany) and the slow growth rate of real GDP (predicted to be 2.1 per cent for the EU in 1999 and even less for France and Germany). The new finance ministers for Germany (Oskar Lafontaine) and France (Dominique Strauss-Kahn) argued that central bankers should pay as much attention to employment as to inflation, that greater control should be exercised over exchange rates, that labour market 'reforms' should be abandoned and that the tax burden should be transferred from individuals to firms. This new rhetoric was confirmed in Austria in late October 1998 at a summit of EU leaders, who expressed a desire to reduce interest rates, undertake public investment programmes to create employment and change the tax structure. No doubt the British Labour government is experiencing a degree of discomfort in this company because it has adopted a more neoliberal approach than its continental colleagues. In particular it has placed monetary policy, based on a low target inflation rate, in the hands of the Bank of England.

Needless to say the crisis makers are horrified by the shift to the left in Europe. They see it as an attack on the right of the European Central Bank (ECB) to pursue antistrategic neoliberal policies without interference from the people through their elected representatives. Liberty is the enemy of neoliberalism. That bastion of neoliberalism, *The Economist*, reacted predictably to these developments. In an issue entitled 'Europe Swerves Left' (31 October 1998, pp. 15–16), it rejected the idea that governments can do anything positive about unemployment in the longrun (this is the old neoliberal fallacy – see my *Longrun Dynamics*), claiming that 'price stability, not jobs is the only sensible long-term goal', and insisting that the 'real culprit' behind the EU's higher unemployment is not the existing tight money policy but rather 'excessive rigidities in labour and product markets' and that governments should be concerned not with 'job creation through public works' but with existing 'structural weaknesses'. No doubt they breathed a sigh of relief when in March 1999 Lafontaine was dropped from Germany's Socialist–Green government.

While the recent rhetoric of Europe's finance ministers may offer encouragement to their strategists, it remains to be seen whether it will be translated into action. There is a vast chasm between rhetoric and reality in politics, particularly when these political leaders are confronted by a monolithic and hostile body of economic experts. And the crisis makers will redouble their efforts to reassert control over these 'deviant' governments. The only viable alternative body of theory, to neoclassicism – strategy theory recently developed in my social dynamics trilogy – has so far been boycotted by the economics profession. Unless there is a turnaround of this situation through a breaking of ranks, it is highly likely that the crisis makers will regain control over left-wing finance ministers.

Even if countries such as France and Germany do resist the crisis makers and proceed with job-creation schemes, it is doubtful that the strategists will be placated. As explained in Chapters 7 and 8, there is a great difference between Keynesian static-demand policies on the one hand and my strategic-demand policies on the other. Keynesian policies will only be effective if they are combined with strategic leadership aimed at stimulating strategic demand and strategic confidence.

If their leaders fail them, the strategists, in a few years time, will feel as trapped as those in Australia today. This will certainly eventuate if experiments with 'green' policies, particularly in Germany, add to the disruption already caused by neoliberal policies. If the European strategists, who swept aside the conservative governments that were disrupting their dynamic strategies, are disappointed by the left-wing–green replacements, to whom will they turn? As none of the mainstream parties is able to facilitate their objectives they will turn to the underworld of radical politics – to the radical right. This will be the second and final stage in their attempt to overcome strategic frustration.

The radical right is already positioning itself to take advantage of such opportunities. In six Western European countries the radical right, as can be seen from Table 6.1, has captured more than 10 per cent of the national vote. For Austria and Switzerland it exceeds 22 per cent, and for France, Italy and Norway it exceeds 15 per cent. Further, in some regions within these nations the radical right has even gained power. In France, for example, the National Front, established 27 years ago by Jean-Marie Le Pen, now controls the administration of four southern towns, and the more sophisticated Bruno Mégret has recently broken away to form a new National Front Party that will appeal more to mainstream voters than the crudely racist Le Pen. A particularly worrying development in these countries is that support for the radical right has risen significantly during the past decade of neoliberal policy making. For example, in the mid

Table 6.1   Voting strength of far-right parties in selected Western European countries

Country	Year	% of vote	Party
Austria	1995	21.9	FPÖ
	1999	26.9	FPÖ
Belgium	1995	10.1	National Front + Vlaams Blok
France	1997	15.2	National Front
Italy	1996	15.7	National Alliance
Norway	1997	15.0	Progress Party
Switzerland	1999	22.5	Swiss People's Party

Notes: FPÖ = Freiheitliche Partei Österreichs (Austrian Freedom Party).

1980s the radical right attracted only 5 per cent of the national vote in Austria, 7 per cent in Italy and 10 per cent in France. The radical right is on the rise and the next few years will be critical for the future of liberty in Europe.

What of the situation in Japan? Currently that country is at its most vulnerable. Its old technological substrategy has been exhausted and it is in the middle of an interstrategic hiatus. After a remarkable record of longrun economic growth between 1950 and 1990, as the old technological strategy unfolded, Japan experienced negative real GDP growth (–2 per cent per annum) together with a negative rate of inflation (–0.2 per cent per annum). Unemployment is also rising, although the official rate of about 4 per cent belies the real situation. There is considerable *under*employment in Japan as the initial response of employers to the downturn was to reduce the working hours of their staff. As these underemployed workers are now being made redundant, the unemployment rate is rising.

Japanese entrepreneurs, who are exploring new strategic opportunities, urgently need positive strategic leadership. Unfortunately they have been badly let down by their conservative governments, which, like contemporary governments throughout the First World, have lost sight of the need to facilitate the objectives of the new strategists. Japan's plight is worse because it is the first rich country to experience strategic exhaustion while under the influence of the neoliberal vision and policies (but other rich countries will follow). Japanese governments have become susceptible to neoliberal pressure from overseas (the United States, IMF, OECD) as well as domestically (the central bank, bureaucracy, academic economists) to spend very large sums on reforming failed financial institutions. As argued elsewhere, effective reform of financial and other institutions will not be possible until Japan's new technological substrategy begins to unfold and the strategic demand for these institutions can be observed. To do otherwise would not only waste vast sums that could be redirected to strategic purposes, it would also be counterproductive.

In addition to neoliberal 'structural reform', the Japanese government has belatedly attempted to stimulate static demand through large-scale spending on public works and tax cuts. This has been advocated even by some neoliberal experts and journalists (*The Economist*, 26 September 1998, pp. 21–3). The latest stimulus programme, announced on 16 November 1998, is for government expenditure amounting to 24 trillion yen (about $US193 billion), made up of 17.9 trillion yen for public works, 6 trillion yen for tax cuts, and 1 trillion yen for aid to Asia. This upgrades an earlier announcement in April 1998 of a more modest fiscal stimulus of 17 trillion yen.

The response of economic experts to these attempts to stimulate static demand have been mixed, ranging from the claim that it is too little too late to the hard-line neoliberal assertion that Keynesian policies are unable to stimulate economic growth. As I argue in the following chapters, the stimulation of static demand can be effective only if it is combined with a systematic attempt to simultaneously stimulate strategic demand and confidence through the provision of strategic leadership. Because this has not been attempted, the expansion of public spending has been accompanied by an even more rapid reduction in private spending.

The political outlook for Japan is not encouraging. Although the opposition is getting its act together, with the rising Democratic Party and the Communist Party presenting a united front, they appear to be throwing their support behind neoliberal policies of microeconomic reform rather than policies to support the new strategists. Clearly there is no joy for strategists from either the moderate right or the left in Japanese politics. How long will it be, therefore, until the frustrated strategists turn to darker political forces?

Surely we do not have to be concerned about the United States. The United States was booming throughout the 1990s, with respectable rates of growth of real GDP (4 per cent per annum), low rates of unemployment (less than 5 per cent) and low rates of inflation (less than 2 per cent per annum). But the best years may be over. The economy is expected to slow, and it is widely predicted that the annual growth rate of real GDP for the year 2000 will fall to about 3.0 per cent or less. This means that the world's largest economy will begin to experience the economic and political problems that have already emerged in other rich societies, particularly as it is the home of neoliberalism.

The widespread recognition that the United States will be less buoyant in the near future contrasts with the situation a few years ago, when enthusiastic commentators – even Alan Greenspan, Chairman of the Federal Reserve – were claiming that their country had discovered the secret of eternal prosperity – the so-called 'information revolution'. Such comments reflect a total lack of understanding of the real nature of the dynamic process. As we have seen, the realistic dynamic-strategy model shows that economic growth proceeds via a number of linear waves of varying length that are generated by the process of exploitation and exhaustion of dynamic strategies (the great waves of about 300 years) and substrategies (the long waves of 20–60 years). There is no such thing as continuous economic growth, because there is always a hiatus between the old and new substrategies/strategies. The country that began the Great Depression in this way should know better.

Although this interstrategic hiatus, popularly called a recession/depression, will never be completely eliminated, it is the responsibility of governments to reduce its duration by providing appropriate support for the new strategists. While it is not possible to precisely predict the timing of these strategic downturns, a close study of a particular society such as the United States using my dynamic-strategy model would unearth signs of growing strategic exhaustion. This would be reflected in declining strategic capacity, a slowdown in real rates of return for dominant economic activities, deceleration of increments to the dominant technology, and a shift in the balance between profit-seeking on the one hand and speculation and rent-seeking on the other. These strategic changes will also be reflected in a slowdown in rates of economic growth and particularly of inflation, and an increase in unemployment. But of the macroeconomic measures, strategic inflation remains the key. A sure sign of false prosperity is where moderate growth and low unemployment are achieved with a rate of inflation close to zero. It means that this prosperity has been achieved in a nonstrategic way – through a boom in spending due to a resource bonanza, the sale of government assets, or running down household savings – and as such will be ephemeral. There are signs that the recent US boom was financed in this ephemeral way.

None of this will lead inevitably to the frustration of American strategists, provided their government maintains its nerve and is able to provide effective strategic leadership. But if the US government takes its direction from neoliberal economic experts rather than its strategists and increases the rate of interest every time that rates of growth and inflation climb above 2 per cent per annum, it will run the real risk of unleashing the forces of political darkness that reside, contained, in even the most prosperous and democratic societies. If and when this occurs there will be a very real danger that the United States and, hence, the world will witness an end to progress and liberty.

Conclusions

The greatest danger currently facing human civilisation is the collapse of strategic leadership. Unless our governments abandon their neoliberal policies – unless they throw off the influence of the crisis makers – they will derail the industrial technological paradigm and bring progress and liberty to an end. This will be brought about as the frustration of the strategists reaches a threshold level that causes them, in desperation, to abandon mainstream political parties in favour of the radical right. By suppressing their real irrational objectives, the radical right will be able to court the frustrated strategists who can see no other way out of the neoliberal quagmire. To grant substantial power to the political underworld would, however, restrict the liberty of the majority of citizens and suppress it entirely for ethnic and other minorities. Once unleashed, this political extremism would be difficult and very costly to control and even then only in the longer term. This danger will remain for as long as we tolerate the crisis makers in our midst.

7
The Confusion of the Crisis Makers

The crisis makers are convinced they are making a difference to global prosperity and liberty. And of course they are. But not in the way they believe. My point is that the world would be in much better shape today in the absence of neoliberal economic experts. Remember that they have exerted a systematic influence over government policy only since the mid-twentieth century. For the preceding eleven millennia human civilisation managed to survive quite well without them. Neoliberalism, in other words, is an unprecedented experiment undertaken only by Western civilisation in its mature phase. And as I show, it is an experiment that has failed.

In this chapter we need to consider what went wrong with this experiment. What is the fundamental problem with orthodox economic policy making? Essentially, the economic experts are confused about the way modern society works. It is a confusion that is all-pervasive. They are confused about the source of economic and political change, the role of financial institutions, the significance of inflation and the real impact of the various instruments of policy. But, rather than admit this confusion, they hide it behind a highly technical façade that few outsiders are able to penetrate. They hide the fact that there is no sound theoretical foundation for policies that are ad hoc and subject to the vagaries of intellectual fashion. And they hide the deficiencies of their policy making behind excuses about the lack of consistency by politicians, and about the disruption caused by external events such as the current Asian 'crisis'. Hence the frustration of the strategists is, in large part, an outcome of the confusion of the crisis makers.

Neoliberal policy

Neoliberal policy has its origins in a highly technical discipline known as neoclassical economics. Yet despite the mathematical rigour of this body of deductive theory – a powerful tool of *static* analysis – it cannot account for the dynamics of human society. What it is good at doing, as we have seen, is resolving simple issues such as the determinants of the price of popcorn. What it is hopeless at is explaining the big issues, such as the rise and fall of nations, why some nations are rich and others are poor, or even how the current Asian crisis emerged. In order to resolve the real global crisis we need effective policies for the big issues rather than the small ones. Unfortunately neoliberal policy is merely policy for the small issues writ large. It is not surprising, therefore, that it is totally inappropriate. What we need today is systematic policy making based on realistic dynamic theory.

If there is no solid foundation of dynamic theory underlying neoliberal policy, on what is it based? The disturbing answer is that it is based on very little. Neoliberal policy arises largely from a set of value judgments about the superiority of market forces over bureaucratic decision making, and from a set of unverified assumptions about the shape of functional relationships between key economic variables (such as the supposed vertical shape of the aggregate supply curve and of the longrun Phillips curve). As neoliberal policies are not generated by a realistic general model of the way the world works, it is not surprising that they tend to be ad hoc in nature and disconcertingly changeable. It is this quality of 'intellectual flexibility' that enables economists to claim always to be correct after the event despite always being wrong before it. What follows is a review of some of the current eccentricities of neoliberal policy, which would be entertaining if their consequences were not so tragic.

'Inflation is the enemy'

The centrepiece of contemporary economic policy is the determination to eliminate inflation. The rate of inflation has become the yardstick by which economic performance is judged. We are even witnessing the emergence of a rapidly expanding literature on 'targeting inflation'. Ideally, we are told by these economic experts, the 'targeted' rate of inflation should be zero because of its distorting effects on markets. There was even a time, just a few years ago, when central banks in some countries made the achievement of a zero rate of inflation part of the employment contracts of their governors. Today there is a more pragmatic recognition that a zero rate of inflation may be desirable in terms of (neoclassical) theory, but that it is difficult to achieve in practice. Usually central banks adopt an inflation target of 2 to 3 per cent.

The aim of central banks today is to detect the emergence of economic conditions, described as 'overheating', that might lead to a rise in the rate of inflation from, say, zero, and to take 'corrective' action to prevent it from going beyond 2–3 per cent. Once 'overheating' has been eliminated through deflationary monetary policy, it should be possible, they argue, to ease the rate of inflation back to zero. The fear seems to be that if the inflation rate exceeds the predetermined target – which is subject to fashion – it will not only distort markets but will also accelerate out of control to become hyperinflationary.

The implication is that, whenever the economy starts to grow rapidly and begins to place a strain on prices, it needs to be brought back to heel. Whenever the economy begins to grow rapidly we invariably hear cries from the crisis makers that the economy is 'overheating' and must be hosed down. The neoliberal way of doing this is to increase the rate of interest to choke off funds to investors and consumers. And because the crisis makers do not trust politicians to keep their nerve when unemployment rises to a level that disturbs the electorate, as it inevitably will, monetary policy has been placed in the hands of neoliberals who are not responsible to the people. These powerful neoliberals control the central banks that have lobbied for, and gained, considerable independence from the democratic process and, hence, from the dynamic strategists. Essentially the argument boils down to that of the neoliberal expert knowing better than the strategists what is in the latter's best interests. This is the usual self-serving argument adopted by anti-strategists everywhere, including those in centrally determined economies.

What is particularly interesting, of course, is that this view about expert control of monetary policy is an outright contradiction of the neoliberal position on the sanctity of market forces. This glaring contradiction suggests that what the neoliberals really mean is that market forces – the decisions of the people in the market place – should be supreme, *unless they are not in the best interests of the crisis makers.*

The crisis makers have been very effective in ensuring that neoliberal desires take precedence over the desires of the strategists. This success is reflected both in the growth of central banks around the globe and in the growing independence of these organisations. Central bank numbers increased rapidly throughout the world during the second half of the twentieth century. In the 1940s there were fewer than 50 central banks worldwide, but by the century's end there were more than 170 – a 3.6-fold increase in just two generations of neoliberal influence. In itself this is not necessarily a bad thing as central banks can play a useful role by acting as lender of last resort, thereby maintaining confidence in the financial system at times of strategic exhaustion. What is disturbing is that a rapidly growing proportion of the world's central banks have been granted a high degree of independence from the influence of the strategists, together with the authority to depress the rate of inflation to zero.

With central banks dominated by crisis makers, it has been an easy matter to suppress the rate of inflation throughout the Western world: just choke economic growth by increasing the rate of interest. Consumer price rises for the industrialised countries fell from a rate of 14 per cent per annum in the second half of the 1970s – a time when the neoliberals gained firm control of policy making – to just 1.5 per cent in 1998. As this is the average for a large number of countries, some have achieved very low, even negative, inflation rates. In Sweden, Switzerland and Japan the 1998 rate of inflation was negative, while in Austria, Belgium, Canada, France and Germany it was less than 1.6 per cent. Even the main eleven EU countries experienced a negative rate of inflation (–0.4 per cent) during one quarter in 1998. Interestingly, in the same quarter these eleven countries were only able to achieve a rate of growth of real GDP of 0.8 per cent (even less in per capita terms), which produced an average unemployment rate as high as 11.1 per cent. Clearly this highly successful attempt by neoliberal central banks to reduce the rate of inflation to zero (or less) has in many cases disrupted their dynamic strategies, just as I predict in *Longrun Dynamics* (1998).

No doubt some readers will draw our attention to a few individual exceptions to this disturbing experience, such as the United States and Australia. Many, including the leading neoclassical economist Paul Krugman, regard the economic performance of the United States as a 'miracle' and of Australia as a 'near miracle'. In 1998 the United States had a rate of inflation of 1.5 per cent, a rate of growth of real GDP of 3.5 per cent, and an unemployment rate of only 4.6 per cent. This was achieved not through strategic development but by favourable external conditions and a remarkable spending spree by American consumers, who reduced the national saving rate to its lowest level since the Great Depression – in September 1998 it actually became negative – and relied heavily on consumer credit and the profits of stock market speculation. The favourable external conditions, which include a decline in competition from East Asia (particularly Japan and South Korea), a strong dollar and lower oil prices, cannot be expected to last, while the consumption spree will soon exhaust itself. When this occurs economic conditions will deteriorate. An ominous sign is the shift in resources from strategic to speculative activity.

Australia also diverged, at least superficially, from the general experience of rich countries. In 1998 Australia's rate of inflation was 1.3 per cent (negative towards the year's end) and its growth of real GDP was in excess of 4.5 per cent but on the down side it had more than 8 per cent unemployment. If we close our eyes to the unemployment rate, these results certainly appear impressive, particularly in the current global climate. But looking beyond the superficial we find that it was the outcome of good luck rather than good management, and that it is likely to be ephemeral rather than permanent. The good luck, ironically, was an outcome of the Asian 'crisis', which was responsible for the large devaluation of the Australian dollar. This currency devaluation was the product of declining confidence in the Australian dollar in a world of flexible exchange rates. In the past governments have attempted, usually unsuccessfully owing to retaliatory action by the rest of the world, to achieve the same temporary effect through devaluation by decree. The current devaluation has been a great boon to Australian exporters, leading to an expansion of exports (by 4 per cent in 1997–98 and 2 per cent in 1998–99), despite the Asian 'crisis'. In turn this has generated a modest burst of nonstrategic growth that does not require an increase in strategic inflation. Any decline in East Asian markets has been more than compensated for by the expansion of European and North American markets. Also the devaluation, together with preparation for the 2000 Olympic Games and the buoyancy of the stock market, has encouraged a modest spending spree for imported and domestic goods. In both 1997–98 and 1998–99 private consumption in Australia increased, at the expense of aggregate saving, by about 4.5 per cent per annum, which matched the increases in those years of real GDP. Hence the current expansion of this small economy is being driven by the whims of the global gamblers, who are responsible for the temporary, if fortuitous, change in the exchange rate, and of consumers, who are discounting the future and exploiting income windfalls. This 'accidental growth', in contrast to 'strategic growth', cannot last.

As the resulting 'accidental growth' is regarded by the strategists as merely temporary, the response to expanding markets at home and abroad has been to increase productivity rather than investment and employment. The expansion of business investment slowed dramatically in 1997–98 and turned negative in 1998–99, R&D expenditure also fell (from 0.9 to 0.7 per cent of GDP) and employment growth was less than half the increase in real GDP over these years. Once the Australian dollar 'recovers' (which will be encouraged by this improved economic performance), *and assuming the crisis makers retain their present headlock on public policy*, 'accidental growth' will collapse. There can be no sustained economic growth when strategic inflation is constantly under neoliberal attack. Australia is the lucky country rather than the clever country it needs to be in order to pursue a successful technological strategy. Obviously Australia cannot continue to rely on luck, and in view of the low priority its present government gives to the development and implementation of new technological and strategic ideas it will probably continue to slip down the global ladder of living standards. While Australia occupied the top rung in the 1880s it is now precariously balanced on the eighteenth rung. This is what must be expected of a country that has lost sight of strategic leadership.

But is this characterisation of neoliberalism based on a straw man of my own making? A brief review of *The Economist*, that prominent neoliberal journal, will show that it is not. Commenting on the recent suggestion of the (then) new socialist finance minister in Germany, Oskar Lafontaine, that central banks should be concerned with jobs as well as inflation, *The Economist* (14 November 1998, p. 22) asserted:

> The notion that central banks should care as much about output and jobs as they do about inflation reflects a misunderstanding. It starts from the fallacy that a low inflation target will permanently choke growth. Yet the bulk of continental Europe's 11% unemployment, which is Mr Lafontaine's gripe, is not due to insufficient demand caused by high interest rates. Rather it results from structural rigidities in Europe's labour and product markets. A looser monetary policy would have no long-term effects on output and jobs; it would simply push up inflation [called 'the enemy']. That reinforces the case for price stability being the right [pun not intended of course] long-term goal for the ECB [European Central Bank] – and for all central banks.

This typical neoliberal statement is a mixture of faith, disingenuousness and bluff.

There is no neoliberal dynamic theory that links inflation, growth, unemployment, 'structural rigidities' and monetary variables. And without such a general model, statements of the kind expressed by *The Economist* can only be based on faith. The best they can do is to use ad hoc pieces of static 'productionist' (neoclassical) theory, which has little or no relevance to real-world dynamics, to support these claims. For example, the above assertion that, in the long term, monetary policy can influence prices but not output and employment is based on the totally unrealistic (and, in a dynamic sense, meaningless) *assumption* that the Phillips curve, which allegedly traces out the long-term relationship between inflation and unemployment, is vertical. Hence monetary policy, which produces a movement along this curve, can affect the rate of inflation on the vertical axis but not the rate of unemployment on the horizontal axis. As I explain in the next chapter, this *assumed* relationship has no real-world dynamic existence.

The disingenuousness in the above extract from *The Economist* concerns the claim that a low inflation target will not 'permanently choke growth'. It is deliberately misleading because the very intention of a central bank *is* to choke growth so as to take the heat out of the economy by forcing inflation back to zero. *The Economist* is really saying that central banks only wish to *temporarily* choke growth. When inflation is dead the central bank will release its stranglehold. What they do not understand is that, while the dynamic strategy is alive, the longrun inflation rate will exceed the central bank target. Hence the stranglehold will only be released when what is dead is not just inflation but also society's dynamic strategy. Finally, *The Economist* is bluffing when it calls non-neoliberal views 'fallacies' because it is unable to provide any supporting evidence or dynamic theory.

In the same article *The Economist* (ibid., p. 23) goes even further. It claims that during periods of rapid technological change we should expect prices to fall continuously. *That deflation is a good thing.* Here it is endorsing the recent views of the editor of the financial newsletter, *Grant's Interest Rate Observer*. We are told that:

> In a period of rapid technological change and large productivity gains . . . prices should be falling, just as they did [in Britain] in the late 19th century. This is the benign type of deflation, not the virulent malignant kind seen in the 1930s.

What this argument implies is that there is a longrun inverse relationship between prices and economic growth. The author goes on to draw a comparison between the bull market of today and that of the late 1920s. It is claimed that both periods experienced rapid technological progress together with official monetary policies that propped up product prices with excessive credit that eventually flowed over into the stock market, causing a speculative boom. This Federal Reserve policy of the 1920s is supposed to have contributed to, if not actually caused, the Great Depression.

Echoing James Grant, *The Economist* argues that, in view of this alleged historical experience, central banks should be concerned not only with commodity prices but also with prices on the stock market, and that a new measure of inflation, including both sets of prices, should be constructed and used to prevent an 'overexpansionary' monetary policy from fuelling speculation. *They are arguing, in other words, for an even tighter monetary policy that will 'allow' commodity prices to fall.*

This is a breathtaking argument. Not because of its profundity, but because of its outrageous abuse of historical and empirical method, its gross misinterpretation of reality, and the frightening possibility that some day soon it might be used as a basis for policy.

Misinterpretation of reality on this scale arises when history is used not as a serious source of evidence of reality but as a selective armoury in a propaganda war. We need to set the record straight. The technological hypothesis about prices can only be tested for countries, such as those in Western Europe, that pursued the dynamic strategy of technological change in the late nineteenth century. Countries pursuing the family-multiplication strategy in that period, such as the United States and Australia, were able to reduce prices from time to time by bringing underused resources into the production process – by occasional resource bonanzas. In the case of Britain, during the late nineteenth century prices fell not because this was a time of 'rapid technological progress' but because Britain's technological substrategy began to stagnate and decline between 1870 and the Second World War. This is reflected in the progressive decline in the rate of economic growth (of real GDP per capita) of Britain over these eight decades (Table 7.1).

If we examine the relationship between prices and economic growth in a careful empirical way – as I have attempted in a series of books, including *Economics without Time* (1993, pp. 256, 266) and *The Ephemeral Civilization* (1997, pp. 275–7) – it becomes clear that throughout the past and present, prices and real GDP per capita always rise and fall together. Hence in the real world growth and inflation

Table 7.1 British growth rates (GDP per capita), 1801–1987

Period	% p.a.
1801–1830	0.5
1830–1870	1.4
1870–1913	1.0
1913–1950	0.8
1950–1973	2.5
1973–1987	1.5

Source: Snooks, *Economics without Time* (London: Macmillan, 1993), p. 247.

are positively rather than inversely related. The reason for this, as shown by the dynamic-strategy model, is that economic growth is driven by strategic demand, not by supply-side variables such as technological progress. There is no such thing in reality as a distinction between 'benign' and 'malignant' price falls. The virtual world of the neoliberal is pure fantasy.

This issue has also been examined in more formal economic terms in *Longrun Dynamics* (1998, ch. 11), where I estimate what I call the **growth–inflation curve** for the very longrun (1370–1994), the longrun (1870–1994), and the shortrun (1961–94). This research shows that prices are a stable, non-accelerating function of the rate of economic growth. This relationship between **strategic inflation** and growth is explained by my general dynamic model. In contrast orthodox economists have no dynamic model to explain their antihistorical argument about an inverse relationship between these variables. It is hardly difficult, therefore, to dismiss the neoliberal myth that inflation is the 'enemy' of modern society.

The other favourite neoliberal myth outlined by *The Economist* is that the Great Depression in the United States was an outcome of the speculative boom on Wall Street that had been fuelled by an overexpansionary monetary policy. In Chapter 3 I provide an explanation of the Great Depression based on systematic historical research. The depression in the United States was an outcome of the exhaustion, by the mid 1920s, of its technological substrategy. It was this technological exhaustion, rather than 'rapid technological progress', that led after 1925 to a decline in strategic rates of return and commodity prices, as well as to a subsequent shift of resources from productive to speculative activities. Commodity prices, in other words, were and are driven by strategic demand. Neoliberals refuse to recognise this reality because, in the absence of a realistic dynamic model, they believe that prices are largely supply driven. And the subsequent boom on Wall Street was fuelled not by monetary policy but by former strategists attempting to maintain their real incomes through speculation.

Hence commodity prices are driven directly by strategic demand rather than inversely by technological change, while the prices of stocks and shares are driven by the changing balance between strategic and non-strategic activities as the dynamic strategy unfolds and is exhausted. The suggestion by *The Economist* that central banks develop inflation indexes that combine the prices of commodities with those of stocks and shares is an outcome of the neoliberal confusion about the relationship between the real and financial sectors. In the real-istic dynamic-strategy model, the financial sector responds to changes in strategic demand. It is not, therefore, an independent cause of economic fluctuations. By combining prices from both sectors, the centrally important strategic demand–response mechanism would be obscured even further, leading to an even tighter stranglehold by the crisis makers on the sources of progress and liberty. The real menace is not inflation but neoliberalism.

'Structural flexibility holds the key'

Orthodox economists do not know why economies grow, stagnate and sometimes collapse. If you doubt this claim, ask them to explain it to you. And do not be fobbed off by technical references to the so-called new growth theory, which tells us nothing about the real-world dynamic process. The claim of the 'new growth' theorists is that they have 'endogenised' (internalised) technological change. But as I explain in *Global Transition* (1999), they have endogenised the wrong variable. Technological change is not the *reason* modern societies grow, merely the *medium* through which a surplus is gener-ated. In the pre-modern world, surpluses were generated not through technological change but through conquest or commerce – through control of an increasing supply of resources rather than a more intensive use of existing resources. What we need to endogenise is the dynamic mechanism that all eras have in common – the mech-anism underlying the dynamic unfolding of the conquest, commerce, and technological strategies. It is the dynamic *mechanism*, not the surplus-generating *medium*, that is essential to our understanding of the way society works.

Because orthodox economists do not understand the dynamics of human society they have no effective policy for encouraging or revit-alising economic growth. Indeed, because they do not understand how to stimulate economic growth they believe that it must be impossible. Hence governments should not even make the attempt. The only legitimate role for governments, we are told, is to remove the alleged barriers to growth. If these supply-side barriers are removed, growth will subsequently emerge unexplained but spontaneously from the private sector. These barriers are 'structural rigidities' in the commodity and factor markets. Neoliberals have a simple faith that greater market flexibility will automatically lead to economic growth and near-full employment. Structural flexibility holds the key to success.

The neoliberal literature overflows with demands for 'structural reform', 'structural adjustment', 'microeconomic reform' and the 'creation of a level playing field'. What this means is that governments should withdraw from active involvement in the market by selling off their businesses, utilities and agencies, and that the public service should be 'down-sized' by retrenching public servants and contracting out work to the private sector (even the security of military barracks is being placed in the hands of private security companies!). It also means breaking down the role of trade unions in labour markets in favour of 'enterprise bargaining', deregulating the financial sector and placing the future of the exchange rate in the hands of global gamblers. The exception to this structural reform and deregulation is central bank control over commodity prices, which they like to claim is the 'enemy'. In the light of my argument about the antistrategic role of independent central banks, this is the first, rather than the last, form of intervention that should be abandoned. But of course that would undermine the self-interest of the neoliberals.

The focus on structural flexibility arises from the supply-side nature of neoclassical economics. If a society is able to set its factor and commodity markets free, we are told, it will achieve the best of all worlds. In this state of neoliberal nirvana the greatest possible efficiency will emerge so that no one can be made better off without making someone worse off. It is the static world of zero-sum games.

All this, of course, is neoliberal fantasy. As I show in the next chapter, institutions, including markets, develop in response to strategic demand rather than neoliberal *interventionism*. In reality it is all part of the strategic demand–response mechanism that lies at the heart of the dynamics of human society.

'It is essential to reduce real wages'

Neoliberals claim that an increase in real wages will erode business profitability, restrain investment and reduce productivity. In turn this will choke off jobs. What they wish to do is to steadily reduce real wages through monetary restraint in the face of a low inflation rate. This reduction in real wages is designed to generate a higher demand for labour and, hence, a lower rate of unemployment. It will, argue the neoliberals, also directly reduce inflationary pressures and allow central banks to pursue a more expansionary policy (even though other neoliberals claim, somewhat inconsistently, that central banks cannot create jobs!).

How do the neoliberals know this? We have seen that they have no realistic dynamic model and that they employ evidence in a highly selective way. In reality the demand for labour is an outcome of the dynamic process rather than the state of *production* relationships, as suggested in neoclassical microeconomics. As I show in the next chapter, the demand for labour is generated by the unfolding dynamic strategy; it is an outcome of strategic demand created by this dynamic process. Neoliberals are blinded to this reality by their static productionist outlook.

Essentially this is a call for a new approach not only to macro-economics but also to microeconomics. The dynamic-strategy approach demonstrates that it is invalid to extrapolate from a productionist microeconomics to the macro level. There is no such thing as an aggregate production function or an aggregate marginal product curve for labour or any other 'factor of production'. The national demand for labour does not depend on the productivity of labour but rather on existing strategic opportunities. It is the strategic demand for labour that is the driving force behind changes in employment and unemployment. The neoliberal argument that national unem-ployment can be reduced by reducing real wages is an outcome of viewing the economy as a giant factory operating in a static world.

Instead of working from microeconomics to macroeconomics, it should be the other way round. This approach would lead to a more realistic form of microeconomics. The firm's demand curve for labour, for example, should be thought of not as the outcome of the mar-ginal product of labour but of the firm's strategic demand for labour determined by the success of its involvement in society's strategic pursuit. We need to abandon the productionist view that the demand for labour is the outcome of the production system. It is this produc-tionist approach that has led to neoliberals advancing supply-side solutions, such as real wage reductions and greater investment in labour skills, to the problem of persistent unemployment. In a dynamic world neither of these measures can reduce unemployment. What reduces unemployment and increases labour skills is an increase in strategic demand for both the quantity and quality of labour arising from the unfolding dynamic strategy.

There are a few other problems with the neoliberal focus on real wages. First, any attempt to reduce real wages when unemployment is high and strategic confidence is low will duly reduce aggregate demand, as Keynes maintained. The 'dynamic' reason is that neoclassical antigrowth policies have already disrupted the dynamic strategy, thereby undermining strategic confidence and reducing strategic demand for labour. In the absence of an expanding strategic demand, businessmen realise that any increase in profits from labour-cost reductions will only be temporary. Second, there is a basic inconsistency (yes, another one!) in arguing on the one hand that markets should be free from interference and on the other hand that nominal wages should be frozen, or even driven downwards. But in a discipline that lacks a general dynamic model – that adopts a shopping-trolley approach to theory – inconsistencies of this type will continue to emerge.

Is Keynesianism dead?

Over the past two decades Keynesianism has fallen from favour in orthodox economic circles. While born-again neoclassical economists never embraced the Keynesian revolution, they felt powerless between the 1940s and 1960s to challenge either its logic or its *apparent* success in creating full employment through its policy of stimulating static demand. Instead they 'infiltrated' the Keynesian camp and attempted to destroy it from within by reinterpreting its central concepts in terms of their own productionist theory. They tried, in other words, to reduce Keynes' broader vision of the economy as a social entity to their own 'vision' of the economy as a giant factory. This attempt to provide Keynesian macroeconomics with microeconomic foundations became known as the 'neoclassical synthesis'. In reality it led to a distortion of Keynes' vision and economic concepts because it proved impossible to reconstruct his macroeconomic theory faithfully by employing productionist building blocks.

The neoclassicists received their chance to push Keynes completely off centre stage when the OPEC oil crisis in the second half of the 1970s led to a rapid increase in both inflation and unemployment. Stagflation did not accord with the simplistic unemployment/ inflation trade-off known as the Phillips curve. Interestingly this concept, which is the creation of naive historicism rather than deductivism, was not sanctioned by Keynes and has no theoretical underpinning. But in the absence of any appropriate theory, it was adopted by the neoliberals. As I show in the next chapter, it is possible to explain stagflation quite easily by employing the dynamic-strategy model.

Because of the persistence of Japan's economic problems, some pragmatic orthodox economists have begun to sanction Keynesian policies in difficult cases. Even *The Economist* (26 September 1998, p. 15), in a recent editorial on Japan's predicament, asserts, without drawing attention to the glaring inconsistency:

> that two things are necessary. A painful [effective medicine must always be painful!] and credible rescue needs to be launched for Japan's banking system; such a rescue will take time. . . . Second, a combination of further fiscal stimulus and an aggressive monetary expansion is needed to revive domestic demand, adding to consumer confidence and buying time while the banking reform is carried out.

Hence Keynesian policies (not mentioned as such) are considered necessary to tide over the Japanese economy until the usual neoliberal policies have time to work. Even the President of the United States, presumably with the approval of his orthodox economic advisers, has recently encouraged the Japanese government to spend its way out of the current difficulties.

This unexpected response by some neoliberals to the Japanese situation appears to be an implicit admission that, when the going gets tough, neoliberal policies cannot be relied upon. It reflects the poverty of neoliberalism. Needless to say the hard-core neoliberals, who regard Keynesian policies as little short of the inspiration of Satan, would never make such an admission no matter how compelling the evidence against them. They assert that Keynesian policies can never succeed; that it is just throwing good money after bad. What Japan needs to do, we are told, is to reform the structure of its economy and to wait. And wait. If that causes pain for the Japanese people, then so much the better, because all effective treatment is supposed to hurt. This is just what the old neoclassical economists advised governments during the Great Depression. And then too the whole world waited and suffered in vain. It was this fruitless waiting and suffering that fuelled the Keynesian revolution half a century ago.

But in reality Keynesianism did not generate recovery from the Great Depression any more than neoliberalism did. While the neoliberals are correct about the long-term ineffectiveness of static-demand stimulation, it is for entirely the wrong reasons. Keynes' *The General Theory* (1936) is only valid in a static world characterised by imperfect institutions. The real world, however, is not static. What led to recovery from the Great Depression was the renewed pursuit of dynamic strategies in various societies around the world.

The first societies to recover were the fascist states of Germany, Japan and Italy because they pursued the obsolete dynamic strategy of conquest – obsolete because, as I show in *The Dynamic Society* (1996), such a strategy in the modern technological era is uneconomical and bound to fail. It is important to realise that these fascist states were not pursuing Keynesian countercyclical policies. Government investment stimulated a response by the private sector that became part of a continuing dynamic process, not because of a Keynesian mechanism but because entrepreneurs expected to receive a high and *continuing* material return on their investment through the booty of conquest. Recovery, in other words, was due to a revival of strategic confidence, even though of a perverted kind.

The problem with Keynesian policy in a real-world depression is that neither the public nor the private sector believes in the reality of a *permanent* return on this public investment. The recovery mechanism, therefore, quickly breaks down. A major flaw in Keynes' *The General Theory* is that it fails to explain the dynamic forces behind investor confidence. Keynes fudges the issue by referring to 'animal spirits' that are, he admits, beyond rational explanation.

By the late 1930s the United States had still not developed a new technological substrategy to replace the old one that had reached exhaustion in the mid 1920s. Despite Roosevelt's New Deal policies, which were Keynesian in spirit, the US economy, which revived partially for a few years, began to head back into the depths at the decade's end. This was only cut short by the outbreak of the Second World War in late 1939 owing to the conquest strategy of Germany. In response the United States, although not officially at war until

December 1941, together with other democratic societies, pursued a defensive form of conquest strategy. Governments and corporations in the Allied countries invested in war infrastructure and war supplies, either for profit (as in the United States from 1939 to 1941) or to prevent the loss of both prosperity and liberty.

Once again, this type of public investment had nothing to do with the ideas of Keynes. Had the United States failed to develop a new technological substrategy – as workshop to the world – in the second half of the 1940s the Great Depression would have intruded into the second half of the twentieth century as many, including Keynes, thought might occur. Hence the eventual recovery from the Great Depression, together with the prosperity of the 'golden age' (1950–73), was the outcome not of Keynesianism but of the renewed unfolding of the industrial technological paradigm, which generated a sustained increase in strategic demand and strategic confidence. The strategic leadership provided by the Truman administration, particularly through the Marshal Plan, played an important role in this process.

Needless to say, neoliberalism had no impact whatsoever on this recovery process. What effect could reforms of the financial sector in the mid 1930s possibly have had on the strategic redirection of the United States during the second half of the 1940s? Clearly none. The time and money devoted to such reforms would have been wasted as there was no way to predict what would be the strategic demand for financial institutions a decade into the future.

In *The General Theory* Keynes attempted to shift the focus of economics from the supply to the demand side – from the bankrupt idea that the economy was a giant factory to the fertile idea that it was a social entity. The reason he did not succeed – why the neoliberals were able to chew him up and spit him out – is that he focused on the wrong sort of demand: on static demand rather than dynamic demand. Keynes' concept of 'effective demand' (or aggregate demand) is no more than the static outcome of strategic demand at a single point in time. What Keynes failed to realise is that there is no point in attempting to stimulate aggregate demand if strategic demand is in decline. The expansionary effect will soon ebb away because the increase in public expenditure will not generate the necessary chain reaction. The private sector is fully aware that, as the expansionary programme is not part of a continuing dynamic strategy, there will be no permanent and continuing return to make the expenditure and risk worthwhile. In other words there will be no recovery of strategic confidence. This is a very different explanation to the static rational-expectations argument put forward rather lamely by the neoliberals.

As argued in the next chapter, governments should provide encouragement and support to the emerging new strategists by subsidising their activities (providing grants for and tax deductions on new strategic R&D), establishing new strategic infrastructure (such as public research and scientific organisations) and negotiating marketing arrangements on their behalf. This is the role – facilitating the objectives of the strategists – that governments have always played. Until now.

Conclusions

Despite their remarkable self-confidence – a self-confidence that arises from intellectual isolation – the crisis makers are confused about the dynamics of human society and what to do when it appears to break down. Both the dominant neoliberal and the banished Keynesian approaches are inadequate. There are a number of reasons for this. First, neither approach possesses a realistic conception of the nature of human society. The neoliberals' distorted vision arises from viewing society as a giant factory dominated by the machine. While it is true that the old Keynesians had a wider vision of the economy as a social entity, they were not aware that it is dedicated to a strategic pursuit. Second, neither approach possesses a general dynamic model of economic and political change. This is critical because it is just not possible to understand and analyse real-world dynamic problems using partial static theory. Both approaches have led to a misdiagnosis of the world's current problems and have prescribed a treatment that will eventually kill rather than cure the patient. Current problems will persist and grow steadily worse, unless the positive harmful neoliberal policies are abandoned completely and the inadequate Keynesian policies are subsumed within the dynamic-strategy approach. The great experiment of Western civilisation with the policy leadership of economic experts has failed. It is crucial that human society does not fail with them.

8
A New Strategic Way

The reason for this exposé of the crisis makers is to clear the ground for the construction of a new way – the strategic way. It is important not to waste this opportunity. To criticise and then fail to create a viable alternative would be pointless. If we are to prevent the growing global crisis from leading to the collapse of Western civilisation it is essential to break with the recent past. The means to do this are at hand. The evidence and dynamic theory for an effective alternative to the current crippling neoliberal policies have already been outlined in the two trilogies – on global history and social dynamics – referred to throughout this work. This chapter outlines the policy principles and practice arising from my dynamic-strategy theory.

The general principles of strategic policy

The adoption of a dynamic and strategic vision of human society brings with it a new way of formulating and evaluating economic and social policy. It is an approach that contrasts starkly with neoliberal policy based on a static, productionist view of reality. The two general issues on which we focus here are the new strategic test of policy and the essential role of strategic leadership.

The efficiency test or the strategic test?

The dynamic-strategy model provides the basis for a new central policy principle, namely maximising the sustainable exploitation of strategic opportunities. This dynamic policy principle contrasts with the static principle of neoliberal policy, which is the maximisation of efficiency (or the achievement of Pareto optimality). The measure of the extent to which strategic opportunities are exploited is called the **strategic test**. It replaces the misleading Pareto efficiency test. Efficiency of production and distribution, therefore, is secondary to strategic development. No matter how efficient a society might be, if its dynamic strategy has been disrupted, derailed or exhausted it will stagnate, decline and even collapse.

The empirical measure of the strategic test is the rate of growth of real GDP per capita rather than the recently popular 'human development' or environmental indexes. Only real GDP per capita is a measure of **economic resilience** or the power to survive and prosper. If a society's current rate of economic growth is significantly lower than that achieved for a comparable period in the exploitation of an earlier substrategy, or is significantly less than that of other societies at similar stages in the pursuit of similar technological substrategies, then it is probably not maximising the sustainable exploitation of its strategic opportunities. In that case it is running the risk of longrun crisis and poverty, which is a hopeless basis for improving either human development or the environment. Strategic policy should be kept separate from, although informed by, other aspects of social policy.

The inflation test or the strategic test?

As we have seen, the neoliberals place a great deal of emphasis on the inflation test of economic policy, despite the fact that this test has no theoretical underpinning or empirical support. In *Longrun Dynamics* (1998, ch. 11) I show that both the real-world evidence and the dynamic-strategy model suggest that, in order to launch a new technological substrategy and to achieve any economic growth at all, it is necessary, on average, to generate a base-level rate of inflation of about 3 per cent. Without this there will be no strategic response and, hence, no sustained economic growth. Further, as the growth rate rises from zero, the rate of inflation must increase steadily and in a stable manner in order to facilitate the strategic demand–response mechanism. For a society pursuing a viable dynamic strategy the rate of inflation will be of a non-accelerating kind. There is, in other words, no danger that this strategic inflation will develop into hyperinflation. That occurs only in societies that have derailed their dynamic strategies, such as Germany in 1923, France during its revolution (1790–6) and America during its war of independence (1776–81) – to name but a few.

As economic growth is not the only determinant of inflation, I have drawn a distinction between the systematic element in price escalation, which I call **strategic inflation**, and the more random elements arising from both exogenous shocks (such as wars, revolutions, epidemics, resource bonanzas/crises) and institutional problems (such as the inappropriate actions of central banks, trade unions and wage-setting bodies), which I call **nonstrategic inflation**. I refer to total price increase as **nominal inflation**.

Not surprisingly we face a problem in distinguishing empirically between strategic and nonstrategic inflation in the real world. It is a problem that has increased during the twentieth century, particularly since the Second World War, owing to the emergence of central banks with discretionary powers of intervention. As the money supply was more directly responsive to market forces before the 1940s, it is in the historical data that the existence of strategic inflation can be observed most clearly for individual countries. Nevertheless, the use of recent cross-section data for OECD countries eliminates some of the nonstrategic influences. We can, therefore, empirically explore the relationship between economic growth and strategic inflation predicted by my dynamic-strategy model. The detailed basis for the following outline can be found in *Longrun Dynamics* (1998).

The **growth–inflation curve** for all OECD countries from 1961 to 1994 (excluding the OPEC crisis years) is presented in Figure 8.1. Before investigating the figure, three matters should be borne in mind. First, the results and interpretations concerning this shortrun growth–inflation curve are very similar to those for the longrun (1870–1994) and the very longrun (1370–1994) curves for Britain, which are discussed at length in *Longrun Dynamics*. Secondly, this is not a full-scale empirical study to establish the existence of the growth–inflation curve, rather it is an exercise to determine whether the growth–inflation predictions of my dynamic-strategy model are consistent with real-world evidence. In other words, no attempt has been made to specify the relationship in a way that will maximise the purely statistical relationship ($\bar{R}^2$) between these two variables. Third, it is particularly important to realise that the static, two-dimensional growth–inflation curve does not represent my dynamic

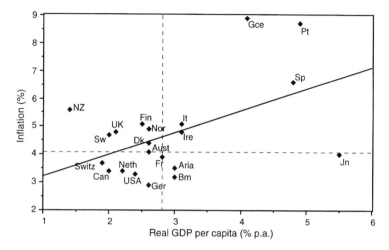

Figure 8.1 The shortrun growth–inflation curve, OECD countries, 1961–73 and 1983–93

Note: The countries included are Australia (Aust), Austria (Aria), Belgium (Bm), Canada (Can), Denmark (Dk), Finland (Fin), France (Fr), Germany (Ger), Italy (It), Japan (Jn), Netherlands (Neth), New Zealand (NZ), Norway (Nor), Sweden (Sw), Switzerland (Switz), United Kingdom (UK), Greece (Gr), Ireland (Ire), Portugal (Pt), Spain (Sp) and USA.

Source: Snooks, *Longrun Dynamics* (London: Macmillan, 1998), p. 155.

model. It is merely an empirical test of one set of predicted outcomes of that more complex dynamic theory.

What does this shortrun growth–inflation curve actually show? It shows that the relationship between the rate of economic growth (real GDP per capita) and the rate of inflation (consumer prices) is positive and stable. It also possesses statistically significant results, passes the usual diagnostic tests, and has similar intercept and slope coefficients to the longrun and very longrun curves. This shortrun curve suggests that, on average, the launching of a successful technological substrategy in the modern world will require a base-level rate of inflation of at least 2.5 per cent per annum, and that the rate of economic growth can be increased to at least 6 per cent per annum with only a modest increase in the rate of inflation in the order of 0.78 percentage points for each additional unit (1.0 per cent per annum) of economic growth. What this means is that, contrary to the conventional wisdom, inflation is a non-accelerating function of economic growth.

By excluding the outliers of Greece and Portugal, for which the nominal inflation data include a greater proportion of nonstrategic elements, the growth–inflation curve becomes less steep, with a base-level rate of inflation of 3.7 per cent, and the addition of only 0.2 percentage points of inflation for each additional unit of economic growth. Inspection of Figure 8.1 shows that not one OECD country during the 1961–94 period (excluding the OPEC oil crisis years), when economic growth was positive and rapid, experienced an average rate of inflation below 3 per cent or above 10 per cent – typically it was between 3.5 and 6 per cent. This is the type of outcome predicted by my dynamic-strategy model; as is the low level of both growth and inflation in recent years.

The most important policy conclusion to emerge from the empirical study of the growth–inflation curve in *Longrun Dynamics* (1998), therefore, is that inflation is a stable, non-accelerating function of economic growth. Erratic bouts of nominal inflation, as occurred in OECD countries between 1974 and 1982, are the outcome of exogenous price shocks and/or institutional mismanagement. Hence, as predicted by my dynamic-strategy model, inflation has no life of its own in a strategically viable society. Only when the dynamic strategy irretrievably breaks down and political institutions collapse, as occurred in Germany in the early 1920s, is inflation likely to rage out of control. One way in which this could occur in the near future is if neoliberal policies aimed at eliminating inflation are actually successful in the longer term. To permanently eliminate inflation would be to derail the dynamic strategy and, hence, to permanently eliminate economic growth. The resulting political chaos would lead, as in the Weimar Republic during 1923, to hyperinflation.

How does the dynamic-strategy model handle the atypical ('miracles') evidence from the United States and Australia of a *shortrun* coexistence of moderate rates of economic growth (nowhere near those of the 1960s) and low rates of inflation? My argument is that a very low to negative rate of inflation is a sure sign that a country's dynamic strategy has been disrupted. In these circumstances a country can continue to grow, *but only in the shortrun*, by running down its savings, borrowing for consumption, enjoying speculative windfalls and fortuitously experiencing favourable external shocks (such as a depreciation of its exchange rate). Such growth is based on misplaced consumer confidence, the sources of which will be quickly exhausted. Sound longrun growth will depend on the abandonment of neoliberal policies and the resumption of the unfolding of a country's dynamic strategy. This will require the acceptance of both strategic inflation and strategic leadership.

On these empirical and theoretical grounds, the neoliberal inflation test must be declared not only invalid but also highly dangerous. It should be rejected by policy makers and replaced with the strategic test, involving rapid and sustained rates of economic growth. Human progress and liberty will continue for as long as we are able to maximise the sustainable exploitation of strategic opportunities.

Economic rationalism or strategic leadership?

Central to any discussion of policy is the role that governments are expected to play. The neoliberal response, as we have seen, is that governments should withdraw from all direct involvement in the economy and restrict themselves to supervising the rules by which society operates and providing a minimal safety net for those who lose their footing in life. We have already noted the inconsistencies between this philosophy and neoliberal intervention in the form of anti-inflationary and structural 'reform' policies. In the light of the dynamic-strategy model and the strategic test of policy, it is clear that we must reject neoliberal philosophy and adopt a new approach to the role of government.

Rather than minimising its involvement, the government should provide positive strategic leadership. What does this involve? In brief, strategic leadership, which is designed to facilitate the objectives of the dynamic strategists, involves investing in strategic infrastructure (including science, research, education, transport and communication facilities) where the social return is expected to exceed the private return; encouraging domestic innovations and their marketing; promoting strategic ideas; spearheading the penetration of new markets by negotiating external trade and technology deals on behalf of its strategists; defending the dynamic strategy at home and abroad; and operating proactively to secure control over external strategic resources (such as oil) and strategic locations. It also involves going far beyond the Keynesian policy prescription of augmenting static demand. This can be done by detecting the *strategic* cause of a major downturn (as in Japan today) and actively assisting in the replacement of exhausted with new technological substrategies. These matters will be discussed in more detail when we review the instruments of strategic policy.

Strategic leadership may, quite justifiably, involve the pursuit of a self-terminating protectionist strategy. This of course is heresy to the neoliberals, but only because they lack sound historical and real-theoretic understanding. Nevertheless, it is essential to distinguish between a protectionist strategy aimed at developing an innovative industrial base and a rent-seeking tactic used to provide monopoly returns for antistrategists in a society not interested in innovation. As I show in *The Ephemeral Civilization* (1997), effective protectionist strategies were pursued by Germany against the economic hegemony of Britain in the early to mid-nineteenth century and the United States against Western-European hegemony in the late nineteenth and early twentieth centuries. In both cases protection was effectively employed *as a first step* in the development of internationally competitive dynamic strategies. By contrast, as I discuss in *Global Transition* (1999), the protectionist policies adopted in most South American countries by rent-seeking interests were ends in themselves. The only way to guard against these rent-seeking interests is to pursue viable dynamic strategies with the assistance of intelligent and informed strategic leadership.

What attention should a strategic leader give to neoliberal concerns about economic stability and internal/external balance? While these issues are important, they should never be allowed to conflict with the systematic and rapid exploitation of strategic opportunities. If we get the strategic issues right, stability will follow. As discussed above, inflation has never been a problem for societies that pursue successful dynamic strategies. As inflation is a stable, non-accelerating function of economic growth, rapid economic change can be pursued without 'overheating' the economy and unleashing the 'monster' of hyperinflation. On the other hand, pursuit of zero nominal inflation – which will result in negative strategic inflation – in the name of stability and order will, if successful, actually derail the dynamic strategy of the Western world and set free the very forces of chaos that the neoliberals appear to fear.

In particular, to grant central banks – organisations not responsible to society's strategists – the independence to suppress inflation at any cost is an invitation to disrupt the dynamic process. Central banks should deal only with *nonstrategic* inflation caused by exogenous events, such as the OPEC oil crisis of the 1970s. But to do so effectively it is essential that they be familiar with the dynamic-strategy model's distinction between and analysis of strategic and nonstrategic inflation. And they should always be subject to the supervision of the strategists.

What about unemployment? A viable dynamic strategy spearheaded by effective strategic leadership will also generate low rates of unemployment in the longer term. This must not be thought of as a trade-off with inflation in the tradition of the Phillips curve. Rather it is an independent outcome of the expansion of strategic demand and strategic confidence that encourage businessmen to regard current profit rates as permanent and, hence, to invest on a long-term basis in exploiting strategic opportunities. When an unfolding technological substrategy falters, it may be necessary to increase government expenditure in relation to revenue, not on unproductive public works as in the Keynesian tradition, but as part of a wider strategic recovery plan. It is necessary to stimulate *strategic* demand rather than *static* aggregate demand.

How does structural reform fit into the strategic policy framework? In a dynamic world, market flexibility is important but secondary to the need to generate an expansion of strategic demand that will create the necessary incentives for institutional change. In other words neoliberal *intervention* in the shape of structural reform is unnecessary, usually quite harmful and certainly a great waste of resources and, therefore, is inconsistent with their own static efficiency criteria. Once again it is a matter of: get the strategic issues right and everything else will follow. The only way to reduce the influence of 'special interest groups' (or rent-seekers) to a minimum is by pursuing a successful dynamic strategy. As I show in *Longrun Dynamics* (1998), the network of special-interest organisations grows and becomes more constricting during periods of strategic exhaustion, or strategic disruption, owing to wrong-headed neoliberal policies, whereas during periods of economic expansion the rates of return on strategic activities are higher than those on rent-seeking games, thereby driving out the special-interest groups.

The instruments of strategic policy

An important objective of this chapter has been to employ the dynamic-strategy model to develop new general policy principles. Detailed policy instruments and programmes can also be constructed by applying the model and the principles to particular countries. Clearly the policy details will vary according to time and place and in particular to the nature of the prevailing economic problems and the sociopolitical environment in which they have arisen. While there is little point in discussing policy instruments in great detail in a general work of this nature, more needs to be said about how to proceed in formulating strategic policy instruments. A few guidelines may be helpful.

'Listen to the strategists'

The reason that modern governments have lost their way is that they have been listening to the wrong people. Instead of consulting neoliberal economic experts, they should have been listening to the strategists. The reason governments emerged at the dawn of civilisation and why their tax-collecting activities have been tolerated ever since is that they are able to facilitate the objectives of the strategists. Wider social and welfare policies have only been adopted during the past century as the majority of people in rich countries have become strategists. It is important, therefore, to retain a clear distinction between the equally important economic policies and social policies. Governments need to get back to basics – they need to listen to the strategists and to acknowledge openly that the great modern experiment with economic experts has failed.

But why should I expect political leaders to listen to what is said in this book? Is not the author setting himself up as an alternative expert? Not at all. All I wish to do is to hold a mirror up to reality. Admittedly it is a mirror of my own making and there will be some flaws in the glass, but all I am saying is, look at history if you wish to know why you should listen to the strategists rather than the experts. The only role of the specialist observer should be to draw attention to the real world and to suggest how this can be done, rather than constructing a virtual world for policy makers to inhabit. The neoliberal adviser has grossly exceeded his proper role as court jester. Because the real world does not resemble his virtual world, the neoliberal expert wants to transform reality through his deforming policies. But it is up to the representatives of the strategists to alter the real world. The court jester has no such mandate.

To what strategists should the government listen? This is a testing question that has been put to me on a number of occasions. It can be answered if we examine the concept of 'strategist' more closely. Earlier I argued that one of the reasons governments have difficulty hearing the creative strategist is that we are all strategists now and we all make a variety of demands on our elected representatives. The task for governments was much easier in the past when the strategists were only a small and powerful proportion of the total population. While he pretended not to hear, King John of England knew what his barons expected of him, and when his deafness persisted they forced him to sign Magna Carta, which in reality was a strategic contract. The same was true of King Charles I, who refused to listen to the strategists of commerce until they placed his head on the axeman's block. Parliament is also a contract between the strategists and their political leader. Today's leaders hear so many voices that they might claim it is reasonable to ignore them all and listen to the simple, if virtual, clarity of the expert instead. But this will not save them any more than did the perverse obstinacy of the failed kings of England.

There is, however, a way of narrowing down the problem. In earlier books I have drawn a distinction between strategists who are 'pioneers' and those who are 'followers' to show how the process of **strategic imitation** works. As this does not suit our purposes here, I will propose another distinction that cuts across these existing categories. For the purposes of strategic leadership the new categories are **surplus-creating strategists** and **surplus-consuming strategists**. The surplus-creating strategist either develops or adopts new strategies in an effort to exploit strategic opportunities (thereby involving both strategic pioneers and strategic followers), while the surplus-consuming strategist (involving mainly followers) demands an increased share of GDP. It is the surplus-consuming strategists, making up the large majority of the people, who distract the government from listening to those who are driving the dynamics of society.

It is to the surplus-creating section of society that strategic leadership should be directed. They are the individuals and groups who
are creating or applying new strategic and technological ideas to
produce new and cheaper goods and services, thereby building new
markets at home and abroad. While all strategists have legitimate
claims on government and should not, indeed cannot, be neglected,
the surplus-consumers must not be the primary focus of *economic*
policy. Their claims should be dealt with through *social* policy, a subject not dealt with in this work. Confusion between the two leads to
the distortion of strategic leadership.

While this approach narrows down the identification problem it
does not resolve it. In order to identify the key surplus-creating strategists and their requirements it may be necessary to establish 'strategist identification' committees for the main sectors of the economy.
The membership of these committees, which would be serviced by
public employees from a new Department of Dynamic Strategy
(DDS), must include not discredited neoliberal experts but the leading strategists. These identification committees would not be policy-
making bodies but merely fact-finding groups. The information they
uncover, which must be published and widely distributed, should be
employed by the DDS to provide the minister with policy options. It
would be up to the government to undertake appropriate strategic
leadership.

Some consideration should be given to the nature and functions of
the Department of Dynamic Strategy, which would become the pre-
mier department in the public service. It is not anticipated that the
establishment of this new department would increase total expenditure on the public service, because the macro-policy sections of
existing departments such as Treasury/Exchequer, Finance, Employment and so on would be cut back through a process of downsizing
and amalgamation. The reorganised remnants of these existing macro-
policy sections would confine their work to the more technical
aspects of framing the budget for strategic leadership that would
be worked out by the DDS, as they would no longer be required to
provide advice on issues such as growth, inflation, employment and
fiscal and monetary policy. Consequently there would be a considerable
reduction in demand for neoclassical economists. Of course there
would still be a role for some of the essential micro-policy areas such
as the investment review section in the Treasury.

Consideration should also be given to the type of training required by public servants considering a career in the DDS. The necessary training would be in the field of what I call 'reality recognition and reconstruction'. To provide this training it would be necessary to establish new university schools/faculties in the new intellectual field of 'dynamic strategy'. These schools would be established under the direction of the DDS, which would be allocated government funds for the purpose. These funds would come largely from the downsizing of existing schools of orthodox economics owing to the reduction in demand for neoclassical economists.

The establishment of these new Schools of Dynamic Strategy would require the development of a new programme of both teaching and research, based on the methodology, concepts, models and empirical work discussed in this book. Existing schools of neoclassical economics would be both reduced in size and reorganised, owing to the marked decline in demand for their product. The remaining small service groups, which would specialise in small technical issues, such as the impact of a tax on the consumption of popcorn, could be attached to the new schools of dynamic strategy.

These proposals should not be regarded as world-shattering. Orthodox schools of economics in Western universities are of very recent origin. They expanded rapidly only after the Second World War when governments, suffering from the fatal forgetfulness, came to rely heavily on the advice of economic experts in the public service. Just as orthodox economics schools rose in response to the great antistrategic experiment, so they will fall with its demise. No doubt this will lead to heated protest from the neoliberals, but the fact is that the world does not owe them a living, particularly as they have caused so much damage and distress. As the neoliberals are so fond of saying: 'There is no such thing as free lunch'. Why should we pay for theirs?

'Provide strategic infrastructure'

An essential requirement of strategic leadership is the provision of strategic infrastructure that cannot be profitably developed by the private sector. This infrastructure, which includes public organisations for research and education in the natural and social sciences, is responsible for promoting the interests of the strategists and, hence, the strategic opportunities of society. In the modern era, dominated by the industrial technological strategy, this infrastructure is necessary for the promotion of society's technological and strategic ideas.

Before examining these very different types of ideas, some consideration should be given to the way this infrastructure could be financed. Funding could be sourced from the sale of existing government non-strategic infrastructure, businesses and utilities to the private sector. There is no strategic reason for governments to own utilities for the supply of water, gas, electricity, transport, communications and waste disposal, except where these services are essential but cannot be provided competitively by the private sector. Indeed in most cases a more effective service could be provided under competitive private ownership. While there was a time when the provision of facilities for railways, telecommunications and air transport could have been regarded as strategic infrastructure – like space facilities today – with the emergence of new technological substrategies based on electronic and biological innovation, that time has passed. Unfortunately many contemporary governments, misled by neoliberalism, are selling off these valuable assets and are wasting the resulting income by unnecessarily turning budget deficits into huge surpluses and by promoting unproductive projects designed to increase the government's electoral support (pork-barrelling). Under the influence of neoliberalism, large budget surpluses are widely regarded as a sign of economic and political virtue. In fact they are a sign that governments are failing to provide strategic leadership, particularly when they are achieved by running down strategic infrastructure in higher education and research. Nations that indulge in these practices will fall far behind in the struggle for progress and liberty.

The distinction between strategic and technological ideas is critical to the issue of strategic leadership. Also, it is central to the analysis of strategic policy, and is the feature that distinguishes my approach from the rest. Throughout my global history and social dynamics trilogies I have argued that human society is not a giant factory as the neoliberal 'productionists' claim, but an organisation devoted to the strategic pursuit. We should therefore, think, in terms of dynamic strategies rather than production techniques. In *Global Transition* (1999) I went further and introduced the concept of the **strategy function**. This has been designed to replace the neoliberal aggregate production function, which is an artificial concept that may have some meaning at the individual factory level but not at the societal level.

The neoliberal idea that society attempts to maximise its economic production from a given set of inputs and the state of technology is a gross distortion of reality. Indeed the neoclassical aggregate production function is a myth and should be abandoned.

My strategy function describes the macroeconomic relationship between the **strategic outcome** of survival and prosperity on the one hand, and the **strategic instruments** by which it is achieved on the other. While this is a static concept, it is determined by the unfolding dynamic strategy driven by the strategic pursuit. Clearly it involves a more complex macroeconomic relationship than that envisaged by the neoliberals. In this functional relationship, strategic outcome, which is measured by real GDP per capita, is an indication not of 'well-being' but of economic resilience – the ability to survive and prosper. And the strategic instruments include both the familiar resources of capital stock (both physical and human), population and technological ideas, and the unfamiliar strategic institutions and organisations, strategic leadership and strategic ideas.

The central feature of the strategy function is **strategic ideas**, because they are responsible for **strategic change** (involving a shift in the strategy function), which increases the prospect of survival and prosperity. Strategic change, therefore, replaces technological change as the central feature of society's strategic pursuit. It is an approach that shows how scarce strategic instruments, such as domestic saving or skilled labour, can be substituted for in the strategic pursuit by more abundant instruments. Of course, while this static expository device is useful in drawing a distinction between strategic and technological ideas, it is not a substitute for the underlying dynamic model.

Strategic ideas determine the ways in which society's strategic instruments can be integrated in order to pursue survival and prosperity. The accumulated flow of strategic ideas can be regarded as the state of **strategic knowledge**, which defines the strategy function. Strategic knowledge is accumulated by organisations at all levels of society to enable them to respond effectively to changing opportunities. These organisations include political parties, bureaucratic departments, educational and research organisations, employer groups, trade unions and, most important of all, households.

It is also important to realise that strategic ideas are not planned in advance, but arise in a pragmatic manner as individuals and their leaders attempt to exploit strategic opportunities in the face of competition for scarce physical and human resources. They are, in other words, a response to changes in strategic demand. These strategic ideas operate at a number of levels, including that of the full dynamic strategy and those of the various substrategies discussed in Chapter 4.

The major outcome of our discovery of the strategy function is the entirely new perspective it provides on technological change. While technology is an important strategic instrument, it is not the key to the dynamic process. That role is played by strategic ideas. While the importance of individual strategic instruments, including technological ideas, waxes and wanes over time, the role of strategic ideas in coordinating the supply response to changes in strategic demand remains absolutely central. This has been the case throughout the history of civilisation. Technological change plays the same dynamic role today as conquest or commerce in the premodern world.

While the detailed discussion of this central new concept can be found in *Global Transition* (1999), the point I want to make here is that government strategic infrastructure must include facilities – such as schools of social science in higher education organisations – for developing and promoting strategic ideas as well as those – such as schools of science and technology – for advancing technological ideas. A society may be at the forefront of technological ideas, but if it falls behind in strategic ideas then it will experience increasing difficulty in competing with other more strategic societies. And these ideas can only be promoted by the government providing the necessary strategic infrastructure. This is a vitally important new distinction that has profound policy implications.

'Focus on strategic ideas'

To enjoy progress and liberty a society will find it essential, as suggested above, both to generate appropriate strategic ideas and to employ them in response to changing strategic opportunities. And the only way to maximise both is through an effective education system capable of providing strategic as well as technical ideas and skills. The major failing of modern systems of education arises from the overshadowing of ideas and skills of a strategic nature by those of a technical nature. I am arguing that the existing balance should be redressed, not by reducing technical facilities but by dramatically improving strategic facilities.

Strategic ideas can best be generated by greater expenditure on the social sciences in universities. It is the government's role to ensure that this expenditure is forthcoming, if not from the private sector then from public bodies. It is not enough for private organisations to provide social science/humanities courses in response to either 'entertainment demand' or 'careerist demand' by students. We have seen how entertainment demand has led in the past few decades to the emergence of 'popular' courses in history, political science and sociology that are little more than fashionable indulgences – courses that cater to the esoteric interests of minority groups, telling them what they want to hear rather than what reality is really like. These courses are neither intellectually demanding nor do they show students how to reconstruct reality. Essentially this contemporary movement in education is a form of storytelling, with more fiction than fact in the plot. While the careerist demands of students may be an effective way of providing relevant programmes for the supply of human capital skills, they will never lead to the development of even more essential strategic skills.

Nothing less than a revolution is required in the social sciences. A revolution driven by a changing balance between the inductive and deductive methodologies. The need for this revolution arises from the failure of deductive social science throughout the Western world to provide a theory of the dynamics of human society. Economics, generally regarded as being at the leading edge of the social sciences, has failed to develop either a satisfactory form of macroeconomics or even a rudimentary form of 'social dynamics', despite having been around for 300 years. The deductive experiment in the social sciences, which emerged from the *Methodenstreit* (battle of the methods) against the inductivists a century ago, has failed to live up to its promise. It is time to begin a new campaign, which the inductivists are now in a position to win.

There is no need here to draw the battle lines for the social-science revolution that I am advocating. The detailed justification can be found in my *The Laws of History* (1998). I will focus here on the policy issues. Universities should be provided with the financial incentives to restructure their schools of social sciences along inductivist lines. This will inevitably involve a reduction in the gameplaying of neoclassical economics and in the storytelling of other disciplines, and it will involve making dynamic-strategy theory central to the social sciences. The existing disciplines will flourish or wither according to their ability to build on this basic foundation of dynamic theory and to contribute to strategic policy.

This restructuring of research and teaching in the social sciences will provide a greater understanding of the forces driving human society, of how to maximise the sustainable exploitation of strategic opportunities, of the type of strategic leadership required in different circumstances, of how sociopolitical institutions (such as democratisation) will change as the dynamic strategy unfolds, of the signs of approaching strategic exhaustion, of the ways to assist the emergence of a new strategy, and of the strategic policies that are required in different circumstances. This new programme in higher education will help us to overcome the fatal forgetfulness that is currently undermining the viability of Western civilisation.

In addition to recognising what is needed to implement strategic change, it is essential that all citizens are able to respond appropriately to it. To ensure this, a strategy-oriented education system at all levels is required. At the present time there is little real direction in education in Western societies. Education has been captured by the surplus-consumers – by the various religious, ethnic, environmental, feminist and gender pressure groups – for the purpose of self-justification and advancement. Even where the state provides some social direction, it is usually based on nonstrategic philosophies, and it is easily hijacked in the name of fashionable 'isms' by the teaching staff. In these circumstances any, apparently enlightened, expansion in government spending on schooling would merely cater for sectional rather than strategic interests. The essential initial requirement is to change the structure of the system of general education.

Naturally it is important that education reflects the varied interests of the participating groups in society, but this should take place within a strategic framework directed towards the survival and prosperity of society as a whole. In this way education would become a more effective strategic instrument than it is under existing educational programmes. The curriculum at all levels, which would be influenced by the changing nature of strategic and technological ideas, should be designed to enable young people to recognise and empathise with their society's strategic objectives, and to encourage them to respond to strategic opportunities in an effective and innovative way. This was a major focus of all earlier successful civilisations. The fashionable antistrategic attack on the real objectives of society should cease to be the norm if we wish to survive and prosper. A strategically oriented people, as all successful societies in the past were aware, is the best asset a society can possess.

'But do not neglect technological ideas'

After strategic ideas, technology is the most important strategic instrument of the modern era. It is essential, therefore, that society be in a position to exploit this instrument as effectively as possible. While this subject has received extensive treatment in the literature, the point that needs to be made here is that the state must provide strategic leadership in the generation and adoption of technological ideas. There are a number of ways in which this can be undertaken, including the provision of technological infrastructure where appropriate, the establishment of incentives where the private sector would be a more effective supplier, and the negotiation of advantageous deals with external interests.

This is not the place to go into details about the type of infrastructure required to promote the search for new technological ideas. What needs to be clarified is the guiding principle: that new technological ideas must support both the unfolding technological substrategy and the search for new substrategies. In this respect governments should invest at the theoretical end of the research spectrum, leaving the applied end to private interests. Public infrastructure, therefore, should be constructed in the areas of pure science, both physical and biological, technical research, and higher education in the natural science and engineering fields. The current neoliberal fashion among governments of withdrawing from the generation of technological (and strategic) ideas will, if it continues much longer, irreparably damage the source of our progress and liberty. Empty government rhetoric about 'adapting to the new frontiers of globalisation', 'maximising intellectual capital' and 'becoming a global leader in innovation and the new technologies' while reducing real funding to these activities will not suffice. Effective strategic leadership in this area is absolutely essential.

It is essential that these public research organisations be run by imaginative administrators who understand the nature of strategic leadership. Too many current 'leaders' of higher education facilities – at both the university and school/faculty levels – are merely failed scholars with a strong sense of self-preservation and self-justification. They are surplus-consumers rather than strategic leaders. In many societies most influenced by neoliberalism, research/education administrators have driven out their best minds and have reduced their organisations to intellectual bankruptcy. Quite deliberately they are substituting commercial physical capital for intellectual human capital by closing down highly skilled research departments and investing the 'savings' in downtown, even off-shore, office space. And the reason is that, while the general community stands to benefit enormously, there are no cash returns to the surplus-consumers from investment in intellectual human capital. It is becoming increasingly difficult to distinguish some universities from commercial investment companies. In these circumstances it will be important for the DDS to have effective representation on the 'election' committees charged with appointing high-level research/education administrators, as the present system is plagued by cronyism.

It is also essential that the scholars and researchers – the surplus-creators who are at the leading edge of new ideas – have an effective voice in designing research programmes and allocating resources. The surplus-consumers, who accumulate resources for empire-building activities, must be weeded out. In recent years of neoliberal-inspired financial stringency there has been a dangerous move by the surplus-consumers in public research/education organisations to attain positions of authority and bleed the surplus-creators to death. This has come about through the replacement of collegial (democratic decision making) with corporate-style management.

The surplus-consumers have been able to hijack the management of universities because, having abandoned serious research (or been incapable of it), they have ample time to play politics, while the real scholars/researchers are, quite properly, preoccupied with their research. These neoliberal-inspired changes are destroying many first-rate research/eduction organisations, because organisations that do not operate in a competitive market of buyers and sellers (as do private enterprise corporations) depend on collegiality – the open criticism of colleagues in a democratic framework – to keep them honest and on the right track. The corporate model, particularly in a period of reduced funding, merely leads to public research organisations being hijacked by surplus-consumers, who then drive out the best researchers/scholars and substitute less able staff pursuing fashionable but nonstrategic research.

In this way many of our best public research organisations have been rendered incapable of contributing to the strategic development of society. They have become a complete waste of taxpayers' hard-won surpluses. It is absolutely essential, therefore, that these public institutions be totally reformed. Owing to the disenfranchisement of many scholarly communities, this can only be achieved from the top down by the minister responsible for the DDS. If not achieved before any future increase in government funding to universities and other research organisations, this money will fall into the hands of the surplus-consumers and will fail to generate the high-quality research expected by these more enlightened political leaders. If society is to continue to prosper, it is essential that the surplus-consumers follow the crisis makers into less vital areas of employment.

There are additional, less direct, methods that a strategic leader can employ to facilitate the emergence of technological ideas. But as they are widely discussed in the literature I will mention them only briefly here.

- A strategically aware government will provide incentives for private investment in new technological ideas through tax concessions on targeted scientific and technological research.
- It will attempt to attract leading-edge companies from other countries to establish high-tech facilities locally through the usual incentives, including tax concessions, low-cost sites and subsidised services.
- It will facilitate connections with companies in other countries in order to accelerate the exchange of technological ideas, finance and highly skilled personnel.
- And it will encourage and facilitate greater interaction between various strategic sectors in society. For example, between industry on the one hand and publicly funded scientific/research/higher education organisations on the other. These publicly funded organ-

isations should increasingly spawn private companies to explore and exploit the commercial opportunities of their research.

While more detailed programmes of technological generation and transfer can be worked out only with the parties concerned, enough has been said to indicate the type of strategic policies that need to be pursued.

Conclusions

There exists today a real global crisis that threatens to put an end to progress and liberty. It is an outcome of the recent emergence of both the fatal forgetfulness and the confusion of the crisis makers. It is, therefore, a crisis, of our own making. And just as we have made it we can unmake it. But it will require a radical change in the way we see our world. We must abandon the distorted neoliberal lenses that we currently employ and adopt the clear view of the new strategic approach. This in turn will require a major reformation of our scientific/research/higher education organisations to deliver not only more effective technological ideas but also, even more importantly, more imaginative strategic ideas to promote the rapid unfolding of the dynamic strategies that are responsible for our progress and liberty. Failure to do so could cause the collapse of Western civilisation.

9
Future Choices and Future Worlds

What does the future hold for modern society? The analysis in this book suggests that we face two fundamental future choices: allow the crisis makers free rein, which will derail the technological strategy and bring progress and liberty to an end; or insist that our governments revert to the age-old policy of strategic leadership, which will revive the technological strategy and ensure sustained human development. Today we are at the crossroads. A very real global crisis is emerging that can only be averted if we make the right choices.

Our future choices will be complicated by the neoliberals themselves. Criticism of their austere policies has been increasing of late, particularly since the IMF exacerbated the economic difficulties in East Asia. In order to save themselves during any recession of their own making, the neoliberals will undoubtedly revert to Keynesian pump-priming policies. They know that their own approach can make recessions but that it cannot unmake them. Neoliberal rhetoric will shift from the evils of inflation to those of deflation. But we should not be fooled. As soon as the economy staggers to its feet, owing to the release of the neoliberal headlock, there will be much earnest talk about economic 'overheating' and 'inflationary pressures', and they will resume their deflationary policies. The bewildered economy will be sent sprawling once more. Neoliberals cannot help themselves, let alone an ailing economy, because they see the world through distorted lenses. It is essential, therefore, that they be relieved of their central policy-making role before Western society falters and its government falls into the hands of the radical right. By then it will be too late.

To remove the crisis makers, a reforming government will need to listen to the strategists once more and reinvent itself as a strategic leader. This transformation will require major reforms of the public service and those organisations capable of generating strategic ideas. The central instrument of the state executive will be the Department of Dynamic Strategy (DDS), which will be charged with identifying the requirements of the dynamic strategists and using these as the basis for strategic policies. Existing economic departments in the bureaucracy, such as Treasury/Exchequer, Finance and Employment, will be dramatically downsized and required to service the DDS. Also central banks must be made accountable to the strategists. No longer can we afford to allow them to pursue independent neoliberal policies. These organisations are the national strongholds of the crisis makers.

The reforms will also need to be extended to those international agents of neoliberalism, the IMF and the World Bank. It is essential that these global organisations respond to the requirements of the emerging strategists and their political representatives in the Third World, rather than impose their deforming 'structural adjustment' programmes on unwilling clients. They should, in other words, assist Third World governments to provide strategic leadership. This assistance will take the form of expertise and resources needed to establish Departments of Dynamic Strategy together with organisations capable of producing strategic ideas relevant to each Third World nation. Technological ideas are more easily obtainable.

This renewal of strategic leadership and the generation of all-important strategic ideas will require nothing less than an intellectual revolution in the study of human society. And the revolutionaries in this transformation will be the inductivists, who draw generalisations from a close and systematic observation of reality. The dominant and reactionary deductivists, who are responsible for the present distorted view of society, will take a back seat. In particular the metaphysical philosophers will serve everyone's best interest by transferring to schools of theology. Philosophical ideas are important, but only when they arise from the inductive study of society rather than from unrealistic deductive minds. The only useful role for deductivists, it seems to me, is in the elaboration of the ideas and concepts that are generated from a systematic study of reality. Only then can we ensure that they focus on important and realistic issues, rather than on trivial and artificial constructs. Only then will sensible policies be formulated.

What will the future hold if governments fail to rediscover their strategic roots? In the short term we will witness the emergence of darker, less rational political forces, similar to those that surfaced in Germany during the interwar years. These forces will certainly curtail individual liberty and, eventually, will derail the prevailing technological substrategies. In the longer term we could experience the collapse of the entire industrial technological paradigm that has been unfolding since Britain pioneered the Industrial Revolution. Paradigm collapse is infinitely worse than substrategy derailment, because it will lead – as the dynamic-strategy model predicts – to the return of the ancient dynamic strategy of conquest, but this time on a truly global scale. This is the ultimate zero-sum strategy whereby the successful warring society gains materially at the expense of the rest of the world. It could spell an end to global progress and liberty for centuries, assuming, of course, that it does not bring on a nuclear winter.

If, on the other hand, Western governments do manage to rediscover their role as strategic leaders and are able to break the power of the crisis makers, how will the world's future unfold? The answer can be found in my model of global strategic transition that is outlined in Chapter 3 and developed fully in my global history and social dynamics trilogies. Over the past two million years the dynamics of human society has been worked out through an interconnected series of technological paradigm shifts. Of these the first was the Palaeolithic (or hunting) revolution about 1.6 million years ago, which involved the extension of human energy through the use of more efficient hunting tools; the second was the Neolithic (or agricultural) revolution about 11000 years ago, which involved the partial substitution of animal, water and wind energy for human energy; and the third was the Industrial Revolution of just over 200 years ago, which involved the substitution of thermal energy derived from fossil fuels for both human and animal energy. During each of these technological eras, which have been occurring at an accelerating rate, the revolution began in a limited region and gradually but steadily spread throughout the world. This is a dynamic process that I have called the global strategic transition (GST).

This global dynamic model, which is based on a close and systematic observation of reality, tells us that if, and only if, governments rediscover their strategic-leadership role, the modern industrial paradigm will continue to unfold until it is finally exhausted some time in the twenty-first century. Following a precarious hiatus, during which intense pressure will be placed on existing technologies, resources and material living standards, a new technological paradigm shift will occur, as it has on three earlier occasions in human history. Only antistrategic despotism could prevent it. When it does take place the modern GST will be essentially complete and the Third World will have been drawn into participation in the existing technological paradigm.

In the future fourth technological revolution, which in *The Dynamic Society* (1996) I call the Solar Revolution, there will be a substitution of solar energy for fossil fuel energy. Thereafter the physical constrains on human progress will be limited only by the flow of energy from the sun. This dynamic process will not only solve the existing problem of underdevelopment and constrained liberty, but it will also release the growing pressure on the environment, just as the Industrial Revolution reduced pressure on organic sources of fuels and materials (particularly forest products) in the late eighteenth and early nineteenth centuries. Major environmental damage is a function not of economic growth, as most ecologists are convinced, but of technological exhaustion.

I remain optimistic that human common sense, when it comes to our material interests, will prevail and the crisis makers will be overthrown. Over the past two million years this common sense has never failed us for long. But in the past we were never dominated by a faceless adversary driven by an ideological vision of the world that is neither shaped by reality nor subject to political processes. This is new territory for humanity. For the future we rely upon governments to realise the error of their recent ways, break free from the bonds of neoliberalism and seek new directions from the strategists. For it is the strategists who have driven human society in the past and who will need to reassert themselves in the future. We must put an end to the reign of the crisis makers before they put an end to progress and liberty. The choice is ours.

Glossary

This Glossary includes the new terms and concepts (arising from my dynamic-strategy theory) dealt with in this book. When a new term or concept is first mentioned in a chapter it appears in bold type. Italics in the Glossary are used to indicate that additional concepts are also defined here.

Antistrategists comprise those ruling elites who assume control of societies during times of strategic crisis and engineer repressive economic and political systems. These command systems are designed to eliminate existing *strategists*, prevent the reemergence of potential strategists and facilitate rent-seeking. Examples of societies dominated by antistrategists include Rome from the time of Claudius, Soviet Russia, Nazi Germany and Maoist China. Control by antistrategists is the outcome of a military-backed takeover by a small band of professional revolutionaries who are able to exploit the chaos that emerges when the new strategists are unable to overwhelm the old strategists during the course of a difficult *strategic transfer.*

Dynamic strategies are those wide-ranging programmes employed by decision makers attempting to maximise the probability of survival and prosperity. In the Dynamic Society these strategies include family multiplication, conquest, commerce and technological change. The adoption of any one of these strategies will depend upon factor endowments and, hence, relative factor prices, and will require investment in specialised infrastructure. This investment generates a stream of positive net returns. Economic growth, therefore, is strategy-led. A dominant dynamic strategy will be pursued until it has been economically exhausted, which will occur when the marginal cost of investment in this strategy equals its marginal revenue. This leads not to collapse but to stagnation. Over time any dominant strategy will consist of a sequence of substrategies by which the economic possibilities of the former are explored. For the modern era these substrategies have been called technological styles.

Economic resilience is the command nations have over material goods and services, and is measured by GDP per capita. It is a measure of society's ability to compete and survive, and should be contrasted with the concept of quality of life, which has little to do with survival in the longrun. Economic resilience is the power of nations, and of human society itself, over longrun survival.

Emerging strategic countries (ESCs) are those nations that are in the process of adopting the modern *dynamic strategy* of technological change. They are in transition from the *global strategic fringe* to the *global strategic core.*

Frustration of the strategists is an outcome of Western governments abandoning their *strategic leadership* role – a role that governments have played throughout the history of human society. Until now. While *strategists* understand intuitively that governments are failing them, they are unable to change the system. They can change governments but not government policies, because all major political parties rely on neoliberal economic advisers. The problem is that neoliberalism is undermining the strategists of the modern world. It is a very dangerous condition, because in their frustration the strategists of some vanguard countries are turning increasingly to the radical right to resolve the current impasse. And it is a condition that will spread throughout the Western world if governments continue to pursue deforming neoliberal policies.

Gamblers' confidence is the antithesis of *strategic confidence*, which is responsible for the trust and cooperation in society necessary to achieve prosperity and liberty. Rather than emerging from the successful pursuit of a viable *dynamic strategy*, it is the outcome of wishful thinking by investors turning increasingly to speculative activities as the dominant dynamic strategy/ substrategy is exhausted. It is gamblers' confidence that drives the frenetic activity on the stock market as economic conditions deteriorate, as was the case in the late 1920s and the mid 1980s, and possibly will be the case in the early years of the twenty-first century. As the confidence of gamblers has no strategic base, it is both irrational and ephemeral. When it finally collapses, speculative activity on the stock market bursts. It is important to realise that financial collapse is the outcome of strategic exhaustion, not the reverse, as the neoliberals would have us believe.

Global strategic core. This consists of a steadily growing number of *strategic countries (SCs)* that constitute the dynamo of global economic change. It is not only responsible for driving the unfolding technological paradigm but is gradually drawing *nonstrategic countries (NSCs)* into its orbit. The latter group of countries constitute the *global strategic fringe*. This growing global interaction between the core and the fringe generates the *global strategic transition (GST)*, which is responsible for what is popularly known as economic development.

Global strategic demand. See *strategic demand*.

Global strategic fringe. This consists of those *nonstrategic countries (NSCs)* and *emerging strategic countries (ESCs)* that are drawn into a spiralling orbit around the strategic core. It is an interaction driven by *global strategic demand* generated within the core, some of which is met by the fringe. This interaction takes place through international trade and factor movements. International trade, therefore, is driven not by comparative production costs – the traditional explanation of neoclassical *productionists* – but by global strategic demand. This constitutes a new theory of international trade.

Global strategic transition (GST) is a complex dynamic process by which an increasing number of *NSCs* are drawn into the vortex of dynamic interaction between the world's most economically advanced nations. This dynamic process is an outcome of the global unfolding of the technological paradigm as *materialist man* in the leading *SCs* explores the existing strategic potential. The resulting transition from *NSC* to *ESC* to *SC* is what is popularly known as economic development.

Growth–inflation curve. This is the empirical reflection of the strategic demand–response mechanism that was first proposed in *Longrun Dynamics* (1998). It is important to realise that this curve describes the relationship between the rate of growth of real GDP per capita and *strategic inflation* (not total or *nominal inflation*). Needless to say, there is a problem involved in filtering out *nonstrategic inflation* from available data. While this can be done roughly for SCs and some ESCs it is impossible for NSCs. Also it is essential to realise that this curve is not the strategic demand–response model, it is merely a rough test of its existence.

Materialist man is a central concept in longrun dynamics. Materialist man is related, yet very different, to the neoclassical concept of *homo economicus*. Rational economic man is not a dynamic force in society, but rather an abstract collection of preferences and rational choices concerning consumption and production. Economic theorists have divorced these behavioural outcomes from more fundamental human motivational impulses. Materialist man, on the other hand, is a real-world decision maker who attempts to survive and, with survival, to maximise material advantage over his lifetime. This does not require perfect knowledge or a sophisticated ability to rapidly calculate the costs and benefits of a variety of possible decision-making alternatives, just an ability to recognise and imitate success. Materialist man includes the strategic pioneers who explore strategic opportunities, and the strategic followers who imitate their success and provide the energy for the unfolding *dynamic strategy*.

Nominal inflation. This is total inflation, composed of *strategic inflation* and *nonstrategic inflation*, a distinction that arises from the dynamic-strategy model.

Nonstrategic countries (NSCs) are nations that have yet to adopt the modern *dynamic strategy* of technological change. They, together with *ESCs*, are the 'underdeveloped' countries of the world.

Nonstrategic inflation is that part of *nominal inflation* not generated directly by the dynamic process. Instead, it is the outcome of exogenous shocks (such as wars, epidemics and resource bonanzas/crises) and institutional problems (such as inappropriate action by central banks, trade unions and arbitration commissions).

Productionists are orthodox economists – namely neoclassicists – who view human society not as a strategic organisation (as in this book) but as a giant factory dominated by the machine. This is because they attempt to analyse society by using the theory of the firm (or factory). Their macroeconomic theory and growth theory are constructed from productionist building blocks, and are exercises in production engineering, not realist economics. Hence the operation and dynamics of human society remain a mystery to the productionists.

Strategic change occurs when new *strategic ideas* are applied successfully by a nation in the *strategic pursuit* of its objectives. In formal but static terms it amounts to a shift of the *strategy function*, which embodies the relationship between *strategic instruments* and the *strategic outcome*. In dynamic terms it is an outcome of the response of strategic ideas to changes in *strategic demand* as the *dynamic strategy* unfolds.

Strategic confidence, which is the outcome of a successful *dynamic strategy*, is the force that keeps human society together. A successful dynamic strategy leads to an effective network of competitive/cooperative relationships, together with all the necessary rules and organisations. In economic transactions, individuals relate directly to the successful strategy and only indirectly to each other. It is not a matter of mutual 'trust' as such – of having confidence in the nature of other individuals – but rather having confidence in the wider dynamic strategy in which they are all involved and on which they all depend. What we know as 'trust' is derived from strategic confidence. Once the dynamic strategy has been exhausted and cannot be replaced, strategic confidence declines and in extreme cases disappears. And as strategic confidence declines, so too does 'trust' and cooperation. Strategic confidence is communicated directly to individuals in a society by the rise and fall in material standards of living and indirectly and less effectively through religious and secular ideology.

Strategic countries (SCs) are those nations that have adopted the modern *dynamic strategy* of technological change. They are the 'developed' countries of the world.

Strategic demand is the central concept in the dynamic-strategy model. It is an outcome of the unfolding *dynamic strategy*, and exerts a longrun influence over both the employment of resources and the institutional and organisational structure of society. Shifts in strategic demand occur as the dominant dynamic strategy unfolds and as one dynamic strategy replaces another. These shifts elicit changes in society's use of resources and its strategic institutions and organisations. At the international level, global strategic demand is generated by the unfolding of the world's current technological paradigm, which in turn is driven by an interaction between the 'developed' countries that make up the *global strategic core*. This global demand elicits a longrun strategic response from 'underdeveloped' countries in the *global strategic fringe*. It leads to economic development, which is part of the *global strategic transition (GST)*.

Strategic hiatus. The interval between two viable *dynamic strategies*/substrategies, usually called a recession or depression, is the outcome of a strategic hiatus rather than a downturn in a continuous business cycle. In other words there is no systematic relationship between two successive dynamic strategies/substrategies, as implied by orthodox trade-cycle theory. The emergence of a new dynamic strategy/substrategy following the exhaustion of an old one is not inevitable. Some societies, such as Rome after AD 180, were unable to make the necessary transition and, therefore, collapsed. The strategic hiatus is a vulnerable time for any society.

Strategic ideas. This new concept is concerned with the alternative ways in which the *strategic instruments* can be brought together to effectively pursue the strategic objective of survival and prosperity. They enable strategic substitution between these instruments in this pursuit. The accumulated flow of strategic ideas is the state of *strategic knowledge*, which defines the *strategy function*. Strategic ideas may have a limited momentum of their own in the shortrun, but over the longer haul they are driven by *strategic demand* generated as individual *strategists* and their leaders attempt to exploit strategic opportunities in the face of competition and scarce resources. Strategic ideas are concerned with how best to exploit these opportunities.

Strategic imitation is the process by which strategic followers emulate the activities of successful strategic pioneers. The followers attempt to imitate not the intellectual mechanism of digital computers but the *dynamic strategies* of successful pioneers. And as the followers successfully imitate the successful pioneers, a new dynamic strategy emerges to challenge the old. This concept is based on the demonstrable fact that the human species is driven not by ideas but by desires. We develop rules not to economise on information and 'trust' but on the world's scarcest resource, intelligence.

Strategic inflation. In the dynamic-strategy model the role of prices is central to the interaction between *strategic demand* and *strategic response*. The unfolding *dynamic strategy* generates an increase in strategic demand that places pressure on existing resources, technologies and institutions, thereby leading to an increase in prices and extraordinary profits. This provides incentives for the strategic response. It is the systematic increase in prices arising from the dynamic process that constitutes strategic inflation. The more erratic impact of exogenous forces (war, epidemics and natural resource bonanzas/crises) and institutional difficulties, is called *nonstrategic inflation*. Total inflation is called *nominal inflation*.

Strategic instruments include the usual factors of production such as land, labour and capital (both physical and human), together with the more novel *strategic ideas*, *strategic leadership*, strategic institutions and strategic organisations. These instruments, which can be substituted one for the other in order to achieve the same *strategic outcome* or can be increased in quantity and/or quality to generate an improvement in outcome, respond to changes in *strategic demand*. In the dynamic-strategy model, as in the real world, strategic demand is the driving force. Say's Law ('supply creates its own demand') exists only in the minds of the *productionists*.

Strategic knowledge, which is the outcome of the accumulation of *strategic ideas*, defines the *strategy function*. A change in strategic knowledge, therefore, causes a shift in the strategy function and, hence, an improvement in *economic resilience*. This knowledge is accumulated by strategic organisations such as households, firms, bureaucracies and governments.

Strategic leadership is a fundamentally important concept in this study. It is essential in facilitating the pursuit of the society's dominant *dynamic strategy*. This role exceeds the minimum laid down by neoliberal advocates of all kinds, including neoclassical economists and constitutional economists such as James Buchanan. The test of strategic leadership is not that of static efficiency (Pareto optimality) but of effective and sustained development of the dominant dynamic strategy (strategic progress). Strategic leadership is also important in generating and maintaining *strategic confidence*, which binds society together through a network of cooperative relationships. It is strategic leadership rather than 'moral leadership' that is essential for the well-being of society. Like 'trust', the moral integrity of society is an outcome of a successful dynamic strategy.

Strategic outcome is the result of the *strategic pursuit*, which embodies the attempt by *materialist man* to maximise the probability of survival and prosperity. In dynamic terms strategic outcome, which can be proxied by real GDP (or Gross Community Income), is generated by the strategic demand–response mechanism, and in static terms it is the outcome of the *strategy function*. It is, therefore, a measure not of 'well-being' but of 'economic resilience' – the ability to survive and prosper.

Strategic pursuit. The central focus of the dynamic model developed in this book is the strategic pursuit. Human society is viewed as a strategic organisation dedicated to the strategic pursuit, in which the pioneering strategists explore the economic potential of the most effective *dynamic strategy* and its substrategies. These strategies have included family multiplication, conquest and commerce in the past, as well as technological change in the present. It is important to focus on the strategic pursuit rather than the means by which this driving force is translated into a material surplus. By focusing instead on the system of production, the *productionists* have failed to come to grips with the dynamic process in their own or any other era.

Strategic response is called forth by changes in *strategic demand* for natural and human resources, capital and technological and institutional ideas. This interaction, which is mediated by increasing prices, gives rise to economic growth. In neoclassical economics the supply side is treated as the active force in society – supply creates its own demand – and in Keynesian economics the supply-side variables are treated as given. But in the dynamic-strategy model, Say's Law is reversed as supply responds to the unfolding *dynamic strategy*. See also *strategic inflation*.

Strategic struggle. The strategic struggle is a contest between various groups in society for control of the sources of society's resources and wealth. Although it employs political instruments it is fundamentally an economic struggle – a struggle for survival and prosperity in the face of scarce resources. This struggle involves a contest between either the new and old *strategists*, or between the strategists and the *antistrategists*. If the transfer of control between the old and new strategists does not occur smoothly, the strategic struggle will lead to civil war or revolution. And if the new strategists are not sufficiently powerful economically to overwhelm the old strategists quickly, the antistrategists may exploit the situation by hijacking the revolution through manipulation of the nonstrategists, and by creating a command system.

Strategic test. The dynamic-strategy model introduces a new central policy principle, namely maximising the sustainable exploitation of strategic opportunities, measured in terms of GDP per capita. But it should be emphasised that this is not equivalent to the optimum growth path idea, because such a path can be identified neither in prospect nor retrospect. In the dynamic-strategy model the 'strategic test' replaces the 'Pareto efficiency test' advocated by neoclassical economists (as efficiency of production and distribution is secondary to strategic development), and the 'Wicksell test' advocated by constitutional economists (because it provides the ultimate and measurable basis for 'unanimity and consensus'). It is a test relevant to the longrun as well as the shortrun.

Strategists comprise the dynamic group in society that invests time and resources in pursuing and profiting from one of the four *dynamic strategies*. The strategists are a diverse group. We must distinguish between the strategic pioneers (the more ambitious and risk-taking) and the strategic followers; between the old strategists (supporters of the traditional strategy) and the new strategists (supporters of the emerging strategy); and between the *surplus-creating strategists* and the *surplus-consuming strategists*. While there is synergy between the pioneers and the followers and the surplus-creators and surplus-consumers, the old and new strategists are generally involved in a struggle for control of society's dominant dynamic strategy. This *strategic struggle* is at the core of institutional change and has been responsible for civil wars and revolutions. It can be clearly seen operating in the Third World today (particularly in Indonesia).

Strategy function. This function describes the relationship between the *strategic outcome* of survival and prosperity and the *strategic instruments* by which it is achieved. While it is a static concept – analysing this relationship at a point in time – it is determined by the unfolding *dynamic strategy*. This relationship is more complex than that envisaged by the *productionists*, and it is based on a new vision of human society as an organisation dedicated to the creative pursuit of strategic objectives rather than as a giant factory dominated by the machine.

Surplus-consuming strategists, who make up the large majority of people in modern society, demand from governments, and sometimes receive, an increased share of GDP. In part, they are responsible for preventing governments from listening and responding to those who are driving society – those I have called the *surplus-creating strategists*.

Surplus-creating strategists are those citizens who either develop or adopt new dynamic strategies/substrategies in an effort to exploit economic opportunities. It is to the surplus-creating section of society, therefore, that *strategic leadership* should be directed. While all strategists have legitimate claims on government and should not, indeed cannot be, neglected, the surplus-consumers must not be the primary focus of economic policy. Their claims should be dealt with through social policy. Confusion between the two leads to the distortion of strategic leadership.

Surplus-generating medium. This is the device through which the *strategic pursuit* of *materialist man* is transformed into the material surplus that satisfies his desire to survive and prosper. While the strategic pursuit has existed throughout the entire history of human society, the surplus-generating medium varies with the *dynamic strategy* being pursued. Since the Industrial Revolution this has been the industrial production system, but in pre-modern society it was either the conquest or commerce systems, and in pre-civilisation society it was the hunter–gatherer system. Clearly none of these surplus-generating systems should be viewed as the dynamic core of human society. The reason orthodox economics is unable to satisfactorily analyse the dynamics of human society is that the *productionists* have focused exclusively on the system of production.

Bibliography

Barraclough, Geoffrey, *The Origins of Modern Germany* (New York: Capricorn Books, 1963).

Keynes, J. M., *The General Theory of Employment, Interest, and Money* (London: Macmillan, 1936).

Marx, K., *Capital*, vol. 1: *A Critical Analysis of Capitalist Production* (Moscow: Foreign Languages Publishing House, 1961; orig. pub. 1867).

Schumpeter, J. A., *The Theory of Economic Development: An Inquiry into Profits, Capital, Credit, Interest and the Business Cycle* (Cambridge, Mass.: Harvard University Press, 1934; orig. pub. 1912).

Schumpeter, J. A., *History of Economic Analysis* (ed. E. B. Schumpeter; New York: Oxford University Press, 1954).

Snooks, G. D., *Economics without Time. A science blind to the forces of historical change* (London/Ann Arbor: Macmillan/University of Michigan Press, 1993).

Snooks, G. D., *The Dynamic Society. Exploring the sources of global change* (London and New York: Routledge, 1996).

Snooks, G. D., *The Ephemeral Civilization. Exploding the myth of social evolution* (London and New York: Routledge, 1997).

Snooks, G. D., *The Laws of History* (London and New York: Routledge, 1998).

Snooks, G. D., *Longrun Dynamics. A general economic and political theory* (London/New York: Macmillan/St Martin's Press, 1998).

Snooks, G. D., *Global Transition. A general theory of economic development* (London/New York: Macmillan/St Martin's Press, 1999).

Index

economic history, basis of economic policy in pre-modern world, 29–30; flawed neoliberal version of, 37–8

economic rationalism, *see* neoliberalism

economic recovery, and renewal of strategic demand and strategic confidence, 54; and strategic leadership, 54 (*see also* Great Depression)

economic resilience, defined, 132, 157; and economic growth, 132; and strategic test, 132

economic theory, of 'gameplayers' and 'realists', 31; in history, 6, 19, 22–3, 29–30 (*see also* classical economics; Keynesian economics); neoclassical economics

education, reform of to improve strategic facilities, 145; as strategic instrument, 147; and surplus-consumers, 147; to be strategy-oriented, 147–8 (*see also* higher education)

emerging strategic countries, strategic leadership in, 81–2

emerging strategic countries (ESCs), defined, 157

endogenous growth theory, *see* neoclassical economics, growth theory of

England, *see* Britain

environmental degradation, and economic growth, 8, 156; and technological exhaustion, 156

equilibrium, *see* stasis

ESCs, *see* emerging strategic countries

eternal recurrence, Britain and breaking of, 69, 73; and pre-modern societies, 68; and technological strategy, 68

EU, *see* European Union

European Union, unemployment in member countries, 105–6

family-multiplication strategy, 39, 45; and nomadic society, 58–9; and palaeolithic society, 58; and palaeolithic technological paradigm, 58–9; and prices, 121; strategists and, 58; of USA, 76, 77–8

far right, *see* radical right

fatal forgetfulness, and democratisation, 83, 88; and fragmentation of strategists, 83; and frustration of the strategists, 90; and lack of clarity of strategic objectives, 83–4; of modern governments, 10, 25, 82–6; and need to placate pressure groups, 83; and pursuit of budget surplus, 85, 143; and running down of strategic infrastructure, 84; and unfolding industrial technological paradigm, 83, 88

financial crisis, as global crisis, 2, 2–3, 4, 34–5; in Japan, 11, 35, 52, 109; and real/strategic crisis, 3–4; spillover from East Asia to rest of world, 4, 9, 53–4; and strategic exhaustion, 40, 52–3 (*see also* economic recovery; global crisis; Great Depression)

financial journalists, as popular interpreters of neoliberalism, 27–8

First World, and frustration of the strategists, 105; and radical right, 105

fiscal policy, and deflation of economy, 7, 9, 15; and taxation, 85

four zeros policy, *see* under neoliberalism

France, and Napoleonic conquest strategy, 47; radical right in, 26, 97, 107–8

United States of America
(USA) – *continued*
mega-market, 78, 79, 79–80;
family-multiplication strategy
of, 76, 77–8; frustration of the
strategists in, 111; 'golden age'
of (1950–1973), 42, 80, 129; and
Great Depression, *see* Great
Depression: inflation, economic
growth and unemployment in,
110; as mega-state, 42, 48, 48–9,
49, 50, 68; and participation in
British commerce strategy, 76,
76–7; and protectionist strategy,
137; strategic leadership in,
76–80; strategic leadership in
and Marshal Plan, 80, 129;
strategic sequence of, 76–7;
technological strategy of, 76, 79;
technological substrategies of,
41–2; technological substrategy
of (1890s–1920s), 48, 80;
technological substrategy of
(1940s–1960s), 42, 48, 80; War
of Independence of and strategic
struggle, 77
USSR, *see* Union of Soviet Socialist
Republics

Venice (medieval), breakdown in
strategic leadership in, 66–7;
democratisation in, 67; Doge as
strategic leader of, 66;
exhaustion of commerce
strategy and experiment with
conquest strategy, 65, 67–8;
and Fourth Crusade, 65;
merchant oligarchy as
strategists in, 66–7; return on
investment in commerce
strategy, 64; sociopolitical
institutional framework for
commerce strategy of, 65–6,
67; stages of commerce strategy
of, 64–5; strategic leadership in,
63–8; and strategic sequence,

75–6; strategic struggle in,
66–7; strategists in, 66–7

wages, and demand for labour, 125;
and inflation, 125; monetary
policy and, 124–5; neoliberalism
reduction of, 124–6; and
unemployment, 125
Walras, Léon, 23
Weimar Republic (Germany), and
abandonment of strategic
leadership, 92, 99; and
abandonment of technological
strategy, 95; and antistrategic
policies of President Hindenburg,
94–5; antistrategists in, 94;
hyperinflation in, 40, 93, 132,
135; rent-seeking and, 93–4;
and rise of Nazi Party, 95;
strategic struggle in, 94–5;
strategists in, 92–3; and Treaty of
Versailles and frustration of the
strategists, 92–3, 94, 96
Western civilisation, threat to, 1,
16, 20, 25 (*see also* progress and
liberty, possible end to)
Western Europe, frustration of the
strategists in, 107; as mega-state,
49, 50; move to left and
frustration of the strategists, 97;
move to the left in and rejection
of neoliberalism, 105–7; radical
right in, 107–8; technological
substrategy of (1830s–1870s),
47–8; working classes, as
co-strategists in technological
society, 75; and technological
strategy, 51, 74–5
World Bank, and disruption of Third
World development, 55; and
East Asian 'meltdown', 4–5; and
global crisis, 35; reform of, 154;
and strategic leadership in Third
World, 154; structural
adjustment programmes of, 4–5,
7–8, 9, 17, 82, 154